CHALLENGED
BY

The Old Testament

E. KEITH HOWICK

Other Books by E. Keith Howick

CHALLENGED BY

The Old Testament

E. KEITH HOWICK

WindRiver Publishing
St. George, Utah

Queries, comments or correspondence concerning this work should be directed to the author and submitted to WindRiver Publishing at:

authors@windriverpublishing.com

Information regarding this work or other works published by WindRiver Publishing, Inc., and instructions for submitting manuscripts for review for publication, can be found at:

www.windriverpublishing.com

Challenged by the Old Testament

Library of Congress Control Number: 2004094221
ISBN 1-886249-22-9

First Printing 2004

Printed in the U.S.A. by Malloy, Inc., on acid-free paper

Table of Contents

Challenged by the Old Testament

List of Abbreviations

1 Chron.	The First Book Of The Chronicles
1 Kings	The First Book Of The Kings, Commonly Called, The Third Book Of The Kings
1 Sam.	The First Book Of Samuel, Otherwise Called, The First Book Of The Kings
2 Chron.	The Second Book Of The Chronicles
2 Kings	The Second Book Of The Kings, Commonly Called, The Fourth Book Of The Kings
2 Sam.	The Second Book Of Samuel, Otherwise Called, The Second Book Of The Kings
Amos	Amos
Dan.	The Book Of Daniel
Deut.	The Fifth Book Of Moses, Called Deuteronomy
Eccl.	Ecclesiastes; Or, The Preacher
Esther	The Book Of Esther
Ex.	The Second Book Of Moses, Called Exodus
Ezek.	The Book Of The Prophet Ezekiel
Ezra	Ezra
Gen.	The First Book Of Moses, Called Genesis
Hab.	Habakkuk
Haggai	Haggai
Hosea	Hosea
Is.	The Book Of The Prophet Isaiah
Jer.	The Book Of The Prophet Jeremiah
Job	The Book Of Job
Joel	Joel
Jonah	Jonah
Joshua	The Book Of Joshua
Judges	The Book Of Judges
Lam.	The Lamentations Of Jeremiah
Lev.	The Third Book Of Moses, Called Leviticus
Mal.	Malachi
Micah	Micah
Nahum	Nahum
Neh.	The Book Of Nehemiah
Num.	The Fourth Book Of Moses, Called Numbers
Ob.	Obadiah
Prov.	The Proverbs
Ps.	The Book Of Psalms
Ruth	The Book Of Ruth
Song	The Song Of Solomon
Zech.	Zechariah
Zeph.	Zephaniah

List of Puzzles and Games

Word Searches

Miscellaneous Games

The *Old Testament* is a wonderful collection of ancient books. Enormous quantities of information are contained within its pages, and it literally begins at the *beginning*. The first five books of the *Old Testament* were written by Moses. In the Jewish religion they're called the *Torah*, and represent the foundation of the Jews' religious beliefs and history. Following these five books are books of history, poetry, and the works and writings of God's prophets. However, all of the *Old Testament* books provide us with a marvelous, faith-promoting insight into the creation and God's dealings with man from the beginning of time.

The *Old Testament* foretells the coming of the Messiah, and although the Lord's chosen people only lived the Law of Moses, that Law—coupled with the teachings of the Lord's prophets—became a looking glass through which the coming of the Savior and the record of his New Testament ministry were mirrored. Those who wrote the books of the *Old Testament* were concerned about God, His relationship with us, and our relationship with Him. Their writings reveal the importance of God's teachings, covenants, and commandments. And teaching these subjects—in an enjoyable way—is what this book is all about.

Challenged by the Old Testament uses the King James Version of the Bible as its reference source, not because this version is better than any other version, but because it is the first widely distributed English version of the Bible. Various Christian groups or individuals may prefer another translation of the Bible, but since the King James version is commonly known and readily available, it was my text of choice for this educational activity book.

There are more than twenty-four hundred questions contained in this book. Each question comes from the pages of the *Old Testament*, or in a few instances, from general knowledge about the traditions concerning it. The reader will find several particularly interesting questions on the "Start" and "Finale" pages and in the "Conclusion" of the book, but regardless of where they're located, every question has an answer provided and a scriptural reference to verify the answer. The reference will generally come after the question to allow the reader to find the answer by looking up the scripture—before peeking at the answer. Nonetheless, all answers—both for the games and the questions—can be found in the "Answers" section at the end of the book.

There are twelve sections in this book. Each section contains topical headings and a variety of games, including some for the mathematically inclined (a list of the games is provided after the Table of Contents). You will also find eight special questions interspersed throughout the text that involve some very unusual *Old Testament* stories. The sections, headings, categories, arrangement, and placement of the questions are my own. They are meant to help parents, students, teachers, and ecclesiastical leaders increase their personal enjoyment, as well as to supplement their lessons and other activities.

So have fun. Take the quiz of a lifetime while you enjoy discovering new things about the *Old Testament*. And if you can answer *all* of the questions without peeking, you can consider yourself a scholar indeed.

Happy Quizzing!

In the Beginning.

There are many unique stories and comments in the *Old Testament* that are dispersed throughout the various categories of this book. To whet your appetite, here's a question involving an unusual circumstance in Second Samuel.

1. A battle occurred between the armies of King David and those who followed his rebellious son, Absalom. The battle occurred in the "wood of Ephraim." What does the scripture say "devoured more people that day than the sword devoured?" (2 Sam. 18:8)

Take a guess at this unique answer before you look it up. Here are two more intriguing questions:

2. What are the names of the only two trees mentioned in the Garden of Eden? (Gen. 2:17; 3:22).

3. What relation was Queen Esther to Mordecai the Jew? (Esther 2:7)

Now we can begin in earnest.

I

In The Beginning

4. Eliphaz advised Job not to despise the what, of the Almighty? (Job 5:17)

5. The Psalmist declared that God ruled the raging of the what? (Ps. 89:9)

6. Jeremiah "lamented" that God would have compassion even though he caused what emotion? (Lam. 3:32)

7. What did the Lord command Joshua and Israel to do immediately after Moses died? (Joshua 1:2)

8. By what name was God NOT known to Israel at Moses' time? (Ex. 6:3)

9. After God saved Noah and his family, He established His what, with Noah? (Gen. 6:18)

10. God demonstrated that He was God at Elijah's contest with the priests of Baal by sending down what element from heaven to consume Elijah's sacrifice? (1 Kings 18:38)

11. God told Isaiah that His hand had laid this "structure" of the earth (things are built upon it). (Is. 48:13)

12. The most high God is known by what name in Psalms? (Ps. 83:18)

13. Elijah's contest between gods was between God and whom? (1 Kings 18:24–25)

14. "Who is a God like unto thee," Micah declares, "that pardoneth iniquity" and "deligheth _____. (Micah 7:18)

---

15. According to Amos, God will only reveal his secrets through his what? (Amos 3:7)

16. The Lord declared to Malachi that he loved Jacob and hated whom? (Mal. 1:2–3)

17. Who does it say the Lord sought to kill while he was returning to Egypt from Midian? (Ex. 4:24)

18. Job said that even after death, he would see God in the _____. (Job 19:26)

19. What was created on the first day? (Gen. 1:4–5)

20. Did God command the prophets to speak good things in Jeremiah's time? (Jer. 14:14)

21. From their sojourn in Egypt to the time of Jeremiah the Lord declared that He had sent His servants the _____ to Israel. (Jer. 7:25)

22. Hosea declared that the Lord had a controversy with whom? (Hosea 4:1)

23. What is another name for "I AM," the God of the *Old Testament?* (Ex. 3:14; 6:3)

24. Micah said that the Lord requires three things of us: to do justly, to love mercy, and to walk what? (Micah 6:8)

25. The Lord declared that He hated Esau, and laid his mountains and his heritage _____. (Mal. 1:3)

26. The scripture states that God _____ of the evil He had planned for Nineveh. (Jonah 3:10)

27. Elijah was commanded to stand on the mount before the Lord, but as the Lord passed by, He was NOT in the wind, the fire, nor the what? (1 Kings 19:11–12)

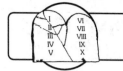

86. After leaving, the creatures returned to Ezekiel as a flash of what? (Ezek. 1:14)

87. Which constellation is mentioned in Job that begins with the letter "O"? (Job 9:9)

88. To what numberless heavenly bodies were the amount of Abraham's future "seed" compared? (Gen. 15:5)

89. When the Lord of hosts reigns, the moon shall be what? (Is. 24:23)

90. What did the people build that included the tower "whose top may reach unto heaven"? (Gen. 11:4)

91. Moses declared that God had multiplied Israel and made her people as numerous as which heavenly constellations? (Deut. 1:10)

92. The constellation Orion is first mentioned in what book?

93. Who did Isaiah say had fallen from heaven? (Is. 14:12)

94. Isaiah records in poetic prophecy that at the Second coming, the stars shall not give their what? (Is. 13:10)

95. Who commanded the sun and the moon to stand still?

96. In poetic imagery, Isaiah declared that when the Lord reigns, the sun shall be what? (Is. 24:23)

SEEING AND HEARING GOD
In The Beginning

Solution on page 279

L	N	H	K	E	F	B	R	L	V	L	T	Q
X	T	X	C	D	I	M	D	M	D	T	Q	C
L	N	I	K	N	R	P	E	N	I	E	L	E
S	O	H	M	Q	E	T	H	V	C	Z	V	S
V	T	K	A	T	R	B	M	A	C	E	W	A
H	R	I	N	G	W	W	F	G	D	P	H	P
K	C	J	L	J	F	J	A	N	T	W	O	P
Z	R	B	M	L	X	R	A	T	T	K	E	H
N	E	L	I	R	S	M	I	B	E	C	K	I
T	N	T	G	M	A	M	V	E	N	R	Q	R
Y	H	D	T	D	K	K	A	A	N	M	S	E
L	B	M	A	M	N	T	R	L	G	D	Q	Y
C	N	M	J	D	V	T	H	E	L	O	R	D

- When Balaam saw God, He was in a what? (Num. 24:4)

- What did Jacob call the place where he saw God face to face? (Gen. 32:30)

- On occasion, God spoke to Moses face to face as a man "speaketh" to his what? (Ex. 33:11)

- Ezekiel described God's appearance as being like this element. (Ezek. 1:27)

- So that Moses could hear God, God spoke to him with His what? (Ex. 19:19)

- How many times does it record that God appeared to Solomon? (1 Kings 11:9)

- Ezekiel declared that God's voice was like the noise of great what? (Ezek. 1:24)

- When Moses, Aaron, Nadab, Abihu, and seventy elders of Israel saw God on Sinai, under His feet there was a stone of what precious substance? (Ex. 24:10)

- When Ezekiel saw the "likeness" of the glory of God, he fell on his what? (Ezek. 1:28)

- When the Lord first called to Samuel, who did Samuel think He was? (1 Sam. 3:5)

- When the Lord passed by Elijah, He was "in" a voice describe as what? (1 Kings 19:12)

- Who did God make in His own image? (Gen. 1:27)

- Who heard the voice of God in the Garden of Eden? (Gen. 3:8)

- Isaiah said that with his eyes, he had seen "the King, ___ _____ of hosts." (Is. 6:5)

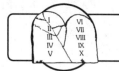
28. In Genesis it states that the living creatures in the waters and the fowls of the air were created on what day? (Gen. 1:20–23)

29. After each day of creation (except the sixth), God sees what he has done and states that it is what? (Gen. 1:4 etc.)

30. What did God call "earth," after he had created it? (Gen. 1:10)

31. What was created on the sixth day? (Gen. 1:26–31)

32. What did God do on the seventh day of creation? (Gen. 2:2)

33. On the fourth day, God created two great what? (Gen. 1:16, 19)

34. During the creation, light was created on which day? (Gen. 1:5)

35. In the beginning, who created the heaven and the earth? (Gen. 1:1)

36. What did God create on the seventh day? (Gen. 2:2)

37. On which day were the sun and the moon created? (Gen. 1:14–19)

38. At the beginning of Genesis it declares that the Spirit of God moved upon the face of the what? (Gen. 1:2)

---

39. What was created on the second day? (Gen. 1:8)

40. The creation story states that, "In the beginning God created" both the heaven and the what? (Gen 1:1)

41. What was created on the fifth day? (Gen. 1:21, 23)

42. During the creation, man was formed from what? (Gen. 2:7)

43. On what day was man created? (Gen. 1:26, 31)

44. What did God divide from both above the firmament and under the firmament? (Gen 1:7)

45. What was dry land called in the creation? (Gen. 1:10)

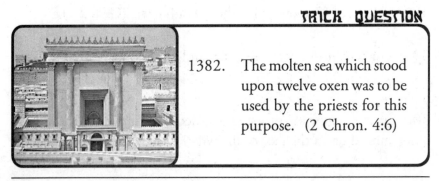

TRICK QUESTION

1382. The molten sea which stood upon twelve oxen was to be used by the priests for this purpose. (2 Chron. 4:6)

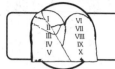

46. Who gave the forbidden fruit to Adam to eat? (Gen. 3:6)

47. What was the name of God's garden? (Gen. 2:8)

48. What did God place in the Garden of Eden to guard the tree of life? (Gen. 3:24)

49. Before creating the woman, God reasoned that it was not good for man to be what? (Gen 2:18)

50. In the Garden of Eden, God said he would place enmity between the serpent and the what? (Gen. 3:14–15)

51. Who made Adam and Eve's first clothes? (Gen. 3:21)

52. Where did Adam and Eve try to hide from God in the Garden? (Gen. 3:8)

53. God cursed the serpent in the garden to travel on its belly and eat what, all the days of its life? (Gen. 3:14)

54. After the transgression in the Garden, what did God put between the woman and the serpent? (Gen. 3:15)

55. What was described in the Garden of Eden as the most subtle beast of the field? (Gen. 3:1)

56. What did Cherubim and the flaming sword guard in Eden? (Gen. 3:24)

57. When could Adam eat freely from the fruit of the Tree of Life? (Gen. 2:16–17; 3:22–24)

58. Why was Adam afraid to face God in the Garden? (Gen. 3:10)

59. In the Garden of Eden, God said he would place enmity between the seed of the woman and the seed of the _____. (Gen. 3:14–15)

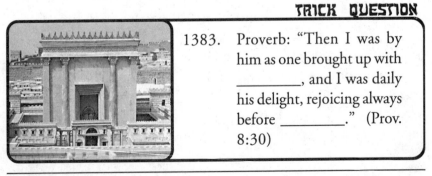

TRICK QUESTION

1383. Proverb: "Then I was by him as one brought up with _____, and I was daily his delight, rejoicing always before _____." (Prov. 8:30)

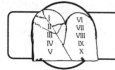

60. The devil quoted from Psalm 91:11–12 to Jesus in which temptation? (Matthew 4:1–11)

61. In Isaiah, Lucifer was called the son of the what? (Is. 14:12)

62. What instrument did David play so that the evil spirit would depart from Saul? (1 Sam. 16:23)

63. What two powerful entities bargained to test Job? (Job 1:7–12)

64. What did the devil promise would open if Adam and Eve ate the forbidden fruit? (Gen. 3:5)

65. When Satan appeared before the Lord (as recorded in the book of Job), he had been going to and fro in the what? (Job 1:7)

66. How long did it take Satan to divest Job of all he had? (Job 1:13–19)

67. In poetic verse, Isaiah declared that the devil wanted to be like whom? (Is. 14:14)

68. What animal did the devil talk through when he spoke to Eve? (Gen. 3:1)

69. Job longed to have God _____ him because of the afflictions imposed by Satan. (Job 6:9)

70. What did the devil promise Adam and Eve they would be like if they ate the forbidden fruit? (Gen. 3:5)

71. In Isaiah's poetic imagery, what word is used to describe the piercing and crooked serpent? (Is. 27:1)

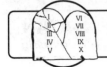

72. When the angel came to speak with Gideon, he first sat himself under what kind of tree? (Judges 6:11)

73. Where did the angel of God remain when the Israelites went through the sea during the Exodus? (Ex. 14:19)

74. What is the name of the angel that told Manoah of Samson's birth? (Judges 13:18)

75. What did Gideon request of the angel to prove he was an angel? (Judges 6:17)

76. What sign did an angel give Gideon to prove he was an angel? (Judges 6:21)

77. When Sarah was promised a son by an angel, Abraham fell on his face and did what? (Gen. 17:17)

78. What did the angel cause to appear between the Egyptians and the Israelites when they were camped near the sea during the Exodus? (Ex. 14:20)

79. What did Lot offer to the men of Sodom in order to protect the "angels" who were staying in his home? (Gen. 19:8)

80. What did the angels do to protect Lot from the men of Sodom who were at his door? (Gen. 19:11)

81. How many men appeared to Abraham in the plains of Mamre? (Gen. 18:2)

82. Jacob _____ with a heavenly being for one entire night before his name was changed to Israel. (Gen. 32:24)

83. In Isaiah (at the time of Hezekiah) an angel smote the camp of what army? (Is. 37:36)

84. How many times did an angel feed Elijah before he went to Horeb? (1 Kings 19:4–8)

85. How did the angel of death know to pass over the homes of the Israelites in Egypt? (Ex. 12:7)

TRUE OR FALSE

1359. Joshua commanded Jordan to stand still in order to assure victory over the Amorites. (Joshua 10:12)

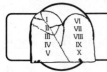

Solution on page 267

Across

2 God declared to Job, "Where was thou when I laid the foundations of the _____." (Job 38:4)

4 Elihu declared to Job that, "Great men are not always _____." (Job 32:9)

5 God asked Job, "Where wast thou when I laid the _____ of the earth?" (Job 38:4)

8 Because of his afflictions, Job wished that God would do this to him. (Job 6:8–9)

9 How many children did Job have before his catastrophe? (Job 1:2)

10 Of all of Job's visitors, who gave him the correct answer? (Job 32)

14 How many of Job's friends and associates came to him after his disasters? (Job 2:11)

16 Job's friends sat with him for seven days and nights without _____ to him. (Job 2:13; 3; 4:1)

19 Job described his friends as what type of comforters? (Job 16:1–2)

20 Job declared that the price of wisdom was above what gems? (Job 28:18)

23 The scriptures state that the Lord answered Job out of this weather anomaly. (Job 38:1)

24 When Job heard of his children's deaths, before he shaved his head he did this to his clothes. (Job 1:20)

25 How many sons did Job have, both before and after his catastrophe? (Job 1:2; 42:13)

26 What personage did Job long to appear before? (Job 22:26; 23:3)

27 According to Job, this is the part of man that God can inspire. (Job 32:8)

Down

1 What did Job have ten of, both before and after his catastrophe and testing? (Job 42:13)

3 Job declared that he knew that his _____ lived. (Job 19:25)

6 Zophar told Job that God was exacting less for Job's _____(singular) than Job deserved. (Job 11:6)

7 What evil son came before God and discussed the activities and character traits of Job? (Job 1:6)

11 Job's first sons and daughters were killed when what structure fell on them? (Job 1:19)

12 The first thing Job "cursed" was the day he was what? (Job 3:1, 3)

13 Eliphaz claimed that the problems Job was having were a result of the _____ the Almighty was giving him. (Job 5:17)

15 How many girls did Job have, both before and after his catastrophe? (Job 1:2; 42:13)

17 Bildad said to Job that God would not cast away a man that was what? (Job 8:20)

18 Satan said that God had placed this barrier around Job to protect him. (Job 1:10)

21 What did Satan cause to afflict Job's body from the crown of his head to the soles of his feet? (Job 2:7)

22 Job lived one hundred and forty years _____ his test from the Lord. (Job 42:16)

TRICK QUESTION

1384. What did the fourth beast in Daniel's vision represent? (Dan. 7:23)

Many of our modern customs, traditions, and expressions come from the *Old Testament*. One of these expressions comes from the celebration of the Day of Atonement.

When the Lord established the Law of Moses for the children of Israel, He also designated certain feast days that Israel was to celebrate each year. Many of their feasts lasted more than one day. One very special day, however, was set aside as a singular day of worship and rest for all the Israelites and any strangers who dwelled among them. This special day was called the Day of Atonement: "For on that day shall the priest make an atonement for you, to cleanse you, that ye may be clean from all your sins before the Lord." A special offering was made to the Lord on this day as an atonement for all the sins of Israel that had been committed during the previous year, thereby allowing the people to enter the new year pure and holy before Him.

During this celebration (between mid September and early October of our calendar), the priest officiating in the temple is required to sacrifice a goat. Two goats chosen for the celebration are brought before him, but only one would be sacrificed—the priest would set the other one free. The officiating priest would cast lots to determine which of the goats would be freed and which would be sacrificed. The priest would then lay his hands upon the head of the goat that was to be set free and "confess over him all the iniquities of the children of Israel and all their transgressions in all their sins, putting them upon the head of the goat." Then the goat was taken to a land that was uninhabited and released.

The Lord commanded that this solemn ritual be observed once each year as an "everlasting statute." He even gave a name to the goat that was to be freed, and from that name comes the expression that we use today to describe a person who is blamed for another person's mistakes.

1409. What was the goat called that received the sins of all Israel upon its head, and was then set free? (Lev. 16:8; see 16:7–22)

II

The Earth Is
The Lord's

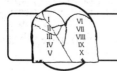

97. Psalm 37 also declares that who, will inherit the earth? (Ps. 37:11)

98. To avoid a curse coming on the earth Elijah would be sent to turn what part of the fathers to the children? (Mal. 4:6)

99. What did the earth bring forth on the third day of creation? (Gen. 1:12)

100. According to Isaiah, the earth became what, because the inhabitants had transgressed the laws, and broken the everlasting covenant? (Is. 24:5)

101. Jeremiah declared that he looked and saw that the earth was without what and void? (Jer. 4:23)

102. Jacob's ladder was set up on earth and reached to where? (Gen. 28:12)

103. The earth was "divided" in the days of whom? (Gen. 10:25)

104. What did the Psalmist say would spring out of the earth? (Ps. 85:11)

105. At the Second Coming, the earth shall what, out of its place? (Is. 13:13)

106. If Elijah does not come, the earth will be smitten with a what? (Mal. 4:6)

---

107. Amos records that he began his prophecy two years before what earth trembling event? (Amos 1:1)

108. In poetic prophecy, Isaiah said the earth would reel to and fro like a what? (Is. 24:20)

109. What was the earth cursed to bring forth because of Adam's sin? (Gen. 3:18)

110. Speaking of the power of the Lord, Nahum stated that the earth is what, at His presence? (Nahum 1:5)

TRICK QUESTION

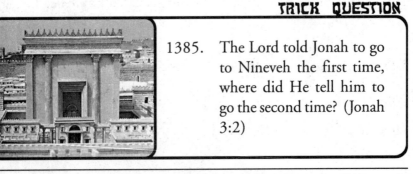

1385. The Lord told Jonah to go to Nineveh the first time, where did He tell him to go the second time? (Jonah 3:2)

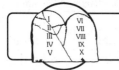

111. A Proverb states that, "he that troubleth his own house shall inherit the" what? (Prov. 11:29)

112. What did God prepare for Jonah that came from the east as Jonah waited for Nineveh's destruction? (Jonah 4:8)

113. What prophet would be taken up to heaven by the Lord in a whirlwind? (2 Kings 2:1)

114. Which direction did the wind come from that parted the sea at the Exodus? (Ex. 14:21)

115. The Psalmist declared that God "stilled" the raging of the waves of the what? (Ps. 89:9)

116. What did Jonah "wish" he had as he waited in the wind and the heat of the sun for Nineveh to be destroyed? (Jonah 4:8)

117. After Elijah's confrontation with the wicked priests of Baal, what did Elijah's servant see the seventh time he looked to the sea? (1 Kings 18:43–44)

118. What happened to the manna each day when the sun waxed hot? (Ex. 16:21)

119. The Lord promised that if the children of Israel would keep His commandments, He would bless them with _____ in due season. (Lev. 26:4)

---

120. What is the word used to describe the strength of the wind that God sent to Jonah while he waited for Nineveh to be destroyed? (Jonah 4:8)

121. What caused Job's eldest son's house to fall in and kill all Job's sons and daughters? (Job 1:19)

1360. The Lord commanded Elijah to go to the brook Chebar during the drought. (1 Kings 17:3)

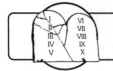

THE FLOOD MATCH GAME
The Earth Is The Lord's

Match the questions on the left with the answers on the right. The solution is on page 263.

A. What did God say man's life span would be after the flood? (Gen. 6:3)

B. How many pair of each specie of fowl were taken into Noah's Ark and saved from the flood? (Gen. 7:3)

C. What did God "asswage" the flood waters with? (Gen. 8:1)

D. How many languages were spoken on the earth before the flood? (Gen. 11:1)

E. Who was Lamech's famous son that was born before the flood? (Gen. 5:28–29)

F. How many pair of "unclean beasts" were taken into Noah's Ark and saved from the flood? (Gen. 7:2)

G. The flood waters prevailed until all the high _____ were covered. (Gen. 7:19)

H. What was the length of time the great flood waters prevailed upon the earth? (Gen. 7:24)

I. What did God command Noah to build? (Gen. 6:14)

J. How long did it rain after Noah was sealed up in the Ark? (Gen. 7:4)

K. Arphaxad was born two years after the flood. Who was his father? (Gen. 11:10)

Seven

An Ark

40 nights

150 days

120 years

Shem

A wind

Noah

Hills

One

Two

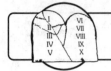
122. Which sea was parted by Moses? (Ex. 13:18; 14:16)

123. As soon as these touched the Jordan river it stopped flowing so that the Israelites could cross over. (Joshua 3:13–16)

124. In the Psalm it declares that when the waves of the sea arise, God will do what, to them? (Ps. 89:9)

125. What river did Elijah strike with his mantle so that the waters would part and allow him to cross? (2 Kings 2:7–8)

126. The Lord (through Jeremiah) said the people had rejected him and hewed them out what, that could hold no water? (Jer. 2:13)

127. How did the Lord (through Moses) supply water to the children of Israel at Horeb? (Ex. 17:6)

128. Who went with Elijah across Jordan on dry ground? (2 Kings 2:8–9)

129. During their travels in the wilderness, the water was bitter when Moses and the Israelites arrived at what location? (Ex. 15:23)

130. How many tribes took their inheritance on the east side of Jordan? (Num. 34:14)

131. What sign did Joshua give the Israelites when they passed over the river Jordan. that God would protect them as they entered the promised land? (Joshua 3: 10, 13)

132. Why did Moses cast a tree into bitter waters? (Ex. 15:25)

133. How many rivers flowed out of the Garden of Eden? (Gen. 2:11–14)

134. What did Elisha's miraculous water look like to the Moabitess. (2 Kings 3:22)

135. Who drank the bitter water at the trial of jealousy? (Num. 5:15–25)

136. With what did Elisha part the Jordan? (2 Kings 2:14)

137. How did the water on both their right and their left appear as the Israelites went through the sea during the Exodus? (Ex. 14:22)

138. What did God use the mist for during the creation process? (Gen. 2:6)

139. What sea was Moses' plague of locusts cast into? (Ex. 10:19)

140. By what river did Ezekiel see his visions? (Ezek. 1:1)

141. To cleanse himself of leprosy, Naaman dipped himself seven times in what river? (2 Kings 5:14)

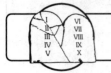

JONAH CROSSWORD
The Earth Is The Lord's

Solution on page 267

Across

2　This is what destroyed the gourd that God had prepared to give Jonah shade. (Jonah 4:7)

4　After Jonah had been in the belly of the fish three days and nights, what did the fish do? (Jonah 2:10)

6　What did the king of Nineveh "sit" in after Jonah called the city to repentance? (Jonah 3:6)

8　A great fish vomited Jonah up on this dry terrain. (Jonah 2:10)

10　How long did the gourd provide shade for Jonah outside Nineveh? (Jonah 4:7)

12　To determine that Jonah was the cause of the tempest, what did the mariners "cast" among themselves? (Jonah 1:7)

16　When God questioned Jonah concerning his anger, Jonah said he did "well" to be angry even unto what? (Jonah 4:9)

17　After Jonah was cast into the sea, what did the sea stop doing? (Jonah 1:15)

18　When the Lord made a gourd to shade Jonah, it states that Jonah was exceedingly _____. (Jonah 4:6)

22　Jonah was vomited out of the fish onto dry land. Who told the fish to do this? (Jonah 2:10)

23　This is what Jonah made for himself while he waited for Nineveh to be destroyed. (Jonah 4:5)

24　How many times was Jonah told by God to go to Nineveh? (Jonah 3:1)

25　While Jonah waited in the heat for

Nineveh's destruction, God prepared this plant to give him shade. (Jonah 4:6)

26 After Nineveh repented, Jonah sat and waited to see what would become of the _____. (Jonah 4:5)

Down

1 Jonah was in this part of a fish when he finally prayed to God. (Jonah 2:1)

2 When Jonah fled, what did the Lord send after Jonah that caused the sea to become disturbed? (Jonah 1:4)

3 During the tempest, what did the ship's captain request of Jonah to help him save his ship? (Jonah 1:6)

5 How many day's journey did Jonah "enter into the city" of Nineveh before he called the people to repentance? (Jonah 3:4)

7 What did the people of Nineveh "put on," after Jonah called them to repentance? (Jonah 3:5–6)

9 Was the fish that swallowed Jonah identified as a whale? (Jonah 1:17)

11 Jonah's reaction to Nineveh's repentance was that he became what? (Jonah 4:1)

13 What was Jonah doing while the sea raged around the mariners? (Jonah 1:5)

14 Jonah requested that the ship's captain cast him into this body of water during the tempest? (Jonah 1:12)

15 The Lord had prepared a great _____ to receive Jonah when he was cast into the sea. (Jonah 1:17)

18 Who did the people of Nineveh believe when Jonah warned them of their imminent destruction? (Jonah 3:5)

19 When Nineveh repented, what did Jonah ask the Lord to let him do? (Jonah 4:3)

20 Jonah said Nineveh would be destroyed (overthrown) in how many days? (Jonah 3:4)

21 The _____ of the Lord commanded Jonah to go to Nineveh. (Jonah 1:1–2)

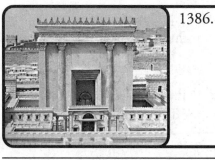

TRICK QUESTION

1386. Male descendants of the tribe of Levi had to be twenty-five to do the work of a priest in the tabernacle. How old did male descendants of Leah's third son have to be to do that work? (Num. 8:24)

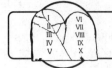
142. What seer stones were in Aaron's breastplate of judgment? (Ex. 28:30)

143. After the Lord put Moses in the cleft of the rock, with what did the Lord cover him? (Ex. 33:22)

144. How many stones did David sling at Goliath? (1 Sam. 17:49)

145. What did Moses see of God from the cleft of the rock? (Ex. 33:22–23)

146. Who made the second set of stone tablets for the ten commandments? (Ex. 34:1)

147. How many stones did Elijah use to build the altar used in the contest between the gods? (1 Kings 18:31–32)

148. What did Moses do with the first stone tablets that contained the Law? (Ex. 32:19)

149. Aaron wore a breastplate of stones. Whose names were on the stones? (Ex. 28:21)

150. How many stones did David select to fight Goliath with? (1 Sam. 17:40)

151. What were the Urim and Thummim located in on Aaron's clothing? (Ex. 28:30)

152. What did the stone cut out of the mountain that smote the man-image in Nebuchadnezzar's dream eventually do? (Dan. 2:35)

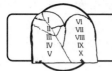
153. Who carried the cluster of grapes back after spying in the promised land? (Num. 13:23; 14:6)

154. What knowledge did the fruit of the forbidden tree contain in the Garden of Eden? (Gen. 2:17)

155. What food did Elisha multiply so that a hundred men could eat and have left overs? (2 Kings 4:42)

156. How long did the angel's food sustain Elijah on his trip to Horeb? (1 Kings 19:8)

157. What fruit did Eve partake of in the Garden? (Gen. 3:6)

158. What was Adam's punishment for eating the forbidden fruit? (Gen. 3:17)

159. What beasts could Israel not eat under the Law of Moses? (Lev. 11:4, 7)

160. According to the requirements of the Law of Moses, could Israel eat the lapwing? (Deut. 14:12, 18)

161. What tree could Adam not eat from in God's garden? (Gen. 2:16–17)

162. Who did Adam blame for making him eat the fruit? (Gen. 3:12)

163. Moses gave the following advise to Israel, and it was later used by Jesus: "Man does not live by what alone, but by every word that proceedeth out of the mouth of the Lord"? (Deut. 8:3)

164. How often did the ravens feed Elijah? (1 Kings 17:6)

165. What would Daniel not eat nor drink so that he would not defile himself? (Dan. 1:8)

166. God described for Moses a ceremony to be held when a woman is suspected of adultery. If the woman is found guilty, she is required to drink bitter water. This ceremony is known today as the trial of _____. (Num. 5:11–24 (18))

167. What did the ravens feed Elijah while he dwelled by the brook Cherith? (1 Kings 17:6)

168. Of things that lived in the waters, Israel could not eat those that did not have what? (Lev. 11:10)

169. What did the Lord cause to rain from heaven each night in order to feed the wandering Israelites? (Ex. 16:4)

170. What sacred bread did David eat? (1 Sam. 21:6)

TRICK QUESTION

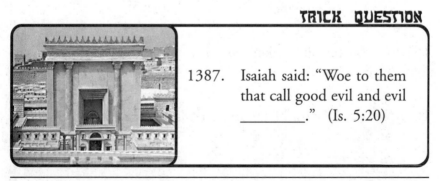

1387. Isaiah said: "Woe to them that call good evil and evil _____." (Is. 5:20)

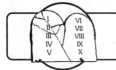
Match the questions on the left with the answers on the right. The solution is on page 272.

A. How many years did Noah live? (Gen. 9:29)

33

B. Nineveh was described as being so large that it took how many days to cross it? (Jonah 3:3)

65

C. Adam lived for how many years? (Gen. 5:5)

69

D. Under the Law of Moses, if a Hebrew servant was bought, he was to be set free after how many years? (Ex. 21:2)

950

930

E. How old was Sarah when she died? (Gen. 23:1)

F. Abraham was told that Israel would be afflicted in captivity for this many years. (Gen. 15:13)

13

3

G. In Daniel's vision, how many symbolic weeks were to expire until Christ's birth? (Dan. 9:25)

15

H. How many years did Solomon reign over Israel? (1 Kings 11:42)

6

I. How old was Enoch when he begat Methuselah? (Gen. 5:21)

J. How many years did it take to build Solomon's temple? (1 Kings 6:38)

127

K. Jeremiah prophesied that Judah would be in captivity for how many years? (Jer. 29:10)

400

L. How many years did David reign over all Israel? (2 Sam. 5:5)

40

M. How many years did it take to build Solomon's house? (1 Kings 7:1)

70

N. How many years did God add to Hezekiah's life? (Is. 38:5)

7

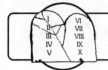

171. How long was it between Jacob marrying Leah and then marrying Rachel? (Gen. 29:28)

172. Where did Jeremiah prophesy that Judah would be held captive for seventy years before the Lord would visit His people? (Jer. 29:10)

173. The Lord said Israel would wander in the wilderness for forty years. How did He determine this number? (Num. 14:34)

174. Who was recorded as the longest living man? (Gen. 5:27)

175. What did the seven years Jacob served for Rachel seem like to him? (Gen. 29:20)

176. When was Jeremiah ordained a prophet? (Jer. 1:5)

177. Which took thirteen years to build, Solomon's temple or his house? (1 Kings 7:1)

178. What month became the first month of the year to the Israelites after the Exodus? (Ex. 13:4; 12:2)

179. How long did it take to divide the sea at the Exodus? (Ex. 14:21)

180. At what hour did the Lord smite the firstborn of Egypt? (Ex. 12:29)

181. Generally speaking, Daniel identified the amount of "time" to the end of time by the phrase "times, time and a _____." (Dan. 12:7)

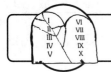
182. Who was cast into the lion's den? (Dan. 6:16)

183. What did Samson observe abiding in the carcass of the lion he had slain? (Judges 14:8)

184. What happened to the "scapegoat" after it received Israel's sins? (Lev. 16:22)

185. What did God do to the lions that were in the den with Daniel? (Dan. 6:22)

186. The Passover lamb at the Exodus was to be selected on which day of the first month of the year? (Ex. 12:3)

187. Who called the she bears forth to destroy the mocking children? (2 Kings 2:22–24)

188. What animal did Goliath compare himself to when confronted by David? (1 Sam. 17:43)

189. What animal killed the disobedient "man of God" in 1 Kings? (1 Kings 13:26)

190. What animal did David order Solomon to ride upon through the city that signified he was to be the next king? (1 Kings. 1:32–33)

191. How long was Jonah in the belly of the great fish? (Jonah 1:17)

192. How many of each "unclean beast" were saved in the Ark? (Gen. 7:2)

193. Who sent the lions among the Assyrian settlers in Israel? (2 Kings 17:25)

194. What judge in Israel killed a lion with his bare hands? (Judges 14:5–6)

195. Elijah's prophesied that at the death of Jezebel, she would be eaten by what animal? (1 Kings 21:23)

196. What beast killed a man for failing to smite a prophet upon request? (1 Kings 20:35–36)

197. In the vision of Zechariah, what was the color of the horses drawing the second chariot? (Zech. 6:2)

198. Forty-two children mocked Elisha because of his bald head; therefore, he cursed the children that they would be torn by two she _____. (2 Kings 2:24)

199. How many yoke of oxen was Elisha plowing with when Elijah found him? (1 Kings 19:19)

TRUE OR FALSE

1361. The second great commandment, love thy neighbor, appears in the *Old Testament* as part of the Law of Moses. (Lev. 19:18)

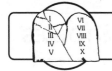

200. What did Jacob place before Laban's cattle to gain ownership of the newborn? (Gen. 30:37)

201. What was Adam told would happen to him if he ate the fruit of the tree of knowledge? (Gen. 2:17)

202. Who made the gourd that shaded Jonah as he watched for the destruction of Nineveh? (Jonah 4:6)

203. What famous trees were to be used in the building of the temple? (1 Kings 5:6)

204. What king grew nails like bird's claws? (Dan. 4:33)

205. What was the first bird sent from the Ark to see if the waters had abated? (Gen. 8:7)

206. Moses saw the bush burn, but it was not _____. (Ex. 3:2)

207. The grass, herbs, and fruit trees were created on which day? (Gen. 1:12–13)

208. Which bird did Noah pull into the Ark with his hand? (Gen. 8:9)

209. The first aprons were made from what? (Gen. 3:7)

Elisha requested that Elijah's power be conferred upon him so that he would be the next prophet in Israel. The sign that this request was granted was that Elijah's cloak was left behind when he was taken into heaven.

Elisha retrieved the cloak and struck the river Jordan with it—just as Elijah had done in the past—and the water parted so that Elisha could walk across on dry ground.

Elisha performed many miracles, but the scriptures report one experience about him that is truly unique. It was brought to my attention one evening when our children were young. I had told the children many times that almost everything in life had a scriptural counterpart. One evening I mentioned this fact again as the family discussed several scriptures. "Oh yeah?" our oldest daughter challenged. "If you can find something about everything in the scriptures, dad, tell us the story of the three bears." She thought she had me. And I have to admit, there isn't a story about three bears in the scriptures. But there is one about two bears.

One day as Elisha traveled from Jericho to Bethel, the scriptures report that a large group of children encountered him. Apparently Elisha was bald, and as children will do, they began to mock and tease him. "Go up, thou bald head; go up, thou bald head," they shouted as he passed by. Perhaps they even pranced along behind him shouting and laughing about his exposed pate.

The scriptures report that Elisha "turned back, and looked upon them, and cursed them in the name of the Lord." Then a most interesting thing occurred. Two (not three) "she bears" came out of the woods and did something to the forty-two children.

Now the questions is:

1410. When the she bears came out of the woods, what did they do to the taunting children as a result of Elisha's curse upon them? (2 Kings 2:23–24)

Who Are The Players?

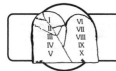

240. What did Joseph's brothers do to get rid of him because of their envy? (Gen. 37:28)

241. How old was Joseph when he died? (Gen. 50:26)

242. What was the source of the blood on Joseph's coat of many colors? (Gen. 37:31)

243. What did Joseph put in Benjamin's sack of corn along with his money? (Gen. 44:2)

244. What did Joseph do when he first saw Benjamin in Egypt? (Gen. 43:30)

245. What did Joseph restore to his brothers' sacks of grain? (Gen. 42:25)

246. What was the name of Joseph's second-born son? (Gen. 41:52)

247. Joseph was sold to what Egyptian? (Gen. 37:36)

248. What was the reason Joseph's brothers went to Egypt? (Gen. 42:5)

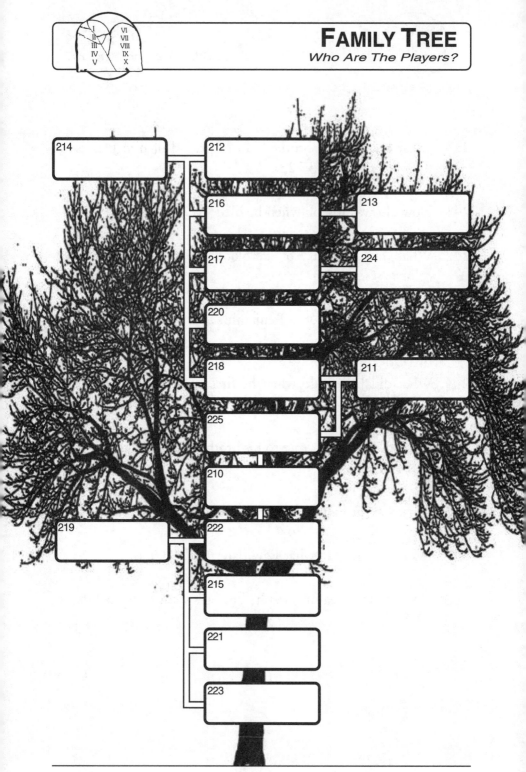

210. What was the name of Obed's son? (Ruth 4:22)

211. Who became the wife of Boaz? (Ruth 4:13)

212. What was the name of Abram's first wife? (Gen. 11:29)

213. Who became the wife of Isaac? (Gen. 24:67)

214. Who was the firstborn son of Terah? (Gen. 11:27)

215. What was the name of Bathsheba's second son? (2 Sam. 12:24)

216. Who was Abraham's second son? (Gen. 21:3)

217. What was the name of Isaac's second son? (Gen. 25:26)

218. Who was the father of Obed? (Ruth 4:13, 17)

219. What was the name of the woman David saw bathing from his roof top? (2 Sam. 11:2–3)

220. What was the name of Jacob's fourth son? (Gen. 29:35)

221. Isaiah provided a sign for Ahaz when he declared that a son would be born of a _____, and His name would be Immanuel. (Is. 7:14)

222. What was the name of Jesse's son who became a king in Israel? (Ruth 4:22)

223. The scepter of Israel was to remain with the tribe of Judah until who should come? (Gen. 49:10)

224. Who was Jacob's first wife? (Gen. 29:21, 23)

225. What was the name the neighbors gave to the first born son of Ruth and Boaz? (Ruth 4:17)

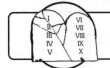
226. When Abraham and his nephew parted, who chose to live near the plain of Jordan, and Sodom and Gomorrah? (Gen. 13:10–11)

227. To whom did Abram pay tithes? (Gen. 14:18–20)

228. Abraham told what two leaders that Sarah was his sister? (Gen. 12:13–15; 20:2)

229. What was the name of Abraham's first son? (Gen. 16:11)

230. Who did Sarah put her "wrong" upon, because she gave Hagar to Abraham? (Gen. 16:5)

231. What did Abraham NOT withhold from God that proved his obedience? (Gen. 22:12)

232. Abraham believed the Lord and it was counted to him for what? (Gen. 15:6)

233. Abraham (Abram) was the first to be called by what name (designating a race)? (Gen. 14:13)

234. How many times did Abraham introduce Sarah as his sister? (Gen. 12:13; 20:2)

235. How old was Abraham when Ishmael was born? (Gen. 16:16)

236. What drove Abraham to leave Canaan and go to Egypt? (Gen. 12:10)

237. How old was Abraham when Isaac was born? (Gen. 21:5)

238. Who stopped Abraham from sacrificing Isaac? (Gen. 22:11–12)

239. What did Sarah ask Abraham to do with Hagar and Ishmael? (Gen. 21:10)

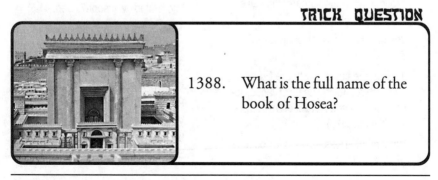

TRICK QUESTION

1388. What is the full name of the book of Hosea?

JOSEPH WORD SEARCH
Who Are The Players?

Solution on page 268

```
E  M  B  A  L  M  E  D  J  T  G  W  N  W  N
R  T  Y  H  S  P  P  R  K  W  H  E  I  I  Q
J  Q  P  L  T  I  B  O  D  K  B  T  M  F  X
K  X  N  P  V  P  M  J  T  U  D  A  W  W  E
F  R  Y  T  K  H  L  E  E  I  J  M  N  P  P
T  G  C  H  T  A  K  R  O  N  P  K  L  D  H
E  X  K  I  N  R  X  M  E  N  B  H  V  K  R
Q  G  G  R  J  A  T  B  R  T  T  K  A  H  A
N  L  R  T  T  O  T  L  R  R  P  R  E  R  I
K  T  C  Y  F  H  M  W  W  N  R  S  D  R  M
T  W  E  N  T  Y  Q  T  O  V  S  T  J  R  Q
Z  A  P  H  N  A  T  H  P  A  A  N  E  A  H
K  T  H  X  T  L  M  F  N  N  F  N  R  L  D
M  C  G  P  M  F  R  A  R  V  J  X  Z  Q  F
P  R  G  L  M  R  M  X  T  J  T  Y  Q  R  L
```

- What was the name of Joseph's first-born son? (Gen. 41:51)

- Joseph was sold into slavery for how many pieces of silver? (Gen. 37:28)

- Which brother of Joseph was left in Egypt as bond for Benjamin? (Gen. 42:24)

- Joseph, for interpreting Pharaoh's dreams, was made greater than all except who? (Gen. 41:40)

- Joseph died in what country? (Gen. 50:26)

- As was the custom with the Egyptian leadership, after the death of Jacob, Joseph commanded that Jacob's body be what? (Gen. 50:2)

- What relation was Asenath to Joseph? (Gen. 41:45)

- Pharaoh changed Joseph's name to what? (Gen. 41:45)

- What was the name of Joseph's son that received the birthright blessing? (Gen. 48. 14, 19)

- Which brother refused to kill Joseph? (Gen. 37:21)

- How many of Pharaoh's dreams were interpreted by Joseph? (Gen. 41:5)

- Joseph, after being sold into Egypt, became the overseer of what Egyptian's house? (Gen. 39:1, 5)

- How old was Joseph when Pharaoh appointed him counselor? (Gen. 41:46)

- What was the name of Joseph's absent brother when the ten came to him in Egypt to buy food? (Gen. 42:4, 13)

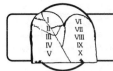

COVENANT MATCH
Who Are The Players?

Match the questions on the left with the answers on the right. The solution is on page 259.

A. What is the name of the locale where Abraham made a covenant with Abimelech? (Gen. 21:31–32)

B. Ezra required the Israelites to covenant to put away both strange children and strange what? (Ezra 10:3)

C. What covenant did Hosea use as a similitude of the covenant between God and Israel? (Hosea 2)

D. Who did David make a covenant with and love as he loved his own soul? (1 Sam. 18:3)

E. What was the "token" of God's covenant with Abraham? (Gen. 17:11)

F. What was the covenant between Israel's spies and Rahab of Jericho? (Joshua 2:14)

G. What "symbol" of the covenant was Moses commanded to build? (Ex. 25:10)

H. What was the "token" of God's covenant with Noah? (Gen. 9:13)

I. What chapter in Genesis initiates the covenant God made with Abraham?

J. What was the unique word Nehemiah used to describe the oath the Levites took when they made a covenant with God? (Neh. 10:29)

K. Ezra required the Israelites to covenant to put away strange wives and strange what? (Ezra 10:3)

L. What chapter in Genesis records the Lord giving the covenant of Abraham to Jacob?

The Rainbow

Genesis 28

Circumcision

Wives

Genesis 12

It was a "curse"

An "Ark of the Covenant"

Children

Jonathan

The marriage covenant

Our life for yours

Beersheba

Challenged by the Old Testament

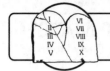

249. Who slept at the king's door instead of in his own bed as ordered by David? (2 Sam. 11:9)

250. Abner was the captain of whose army? (2 Sam. 2:8)

251. How many princes descended from Ishmael? (Gen. 17:20)

252. Saul was afraid because he knew that what Deity had departed from him, and was with David? (1 Sam. 18:12)

253. Who did Esau take as a wife, to displease Isaac? (Gen. 28:8–9)

254. Goliath was the champion of what people? (1 Sam. 17:4)

255. Who did Jonathan love as he did his own soul? (1 Sam. 18:1)

256. When Jeremiah was lowered into the dungeon, what did he sink into? (Jer. 38:6)

257. According to Hosea, the Kingdom of Israel was to be swallowed up by what people? (Hosea 8:8)

258. Absalom was without blemish from his foot to his head, and was known throughout Israel for his what? (2 Sam. 14:25)

259. What office were Aaron and his sons to minister in forever? (Ex. 28:1)

260. What was the name of the son of David whom the Lord loved? (2 Sam. 12:24)

261. God sent Ezekiel to what people? (Ezek. 2:3)

262. To avoid eviction from Canaan, the Gibeonites became what to Israel? (Joshua 9)

263. What nationality was Hagar? (Gen. 16:1)

264. Why did Noah find grace in God's eyes? (Gen. 6:8–9)

265. Who were the first people Abraham told that Sarah was his sister? (Gen. 12:12–13)

TRICK QUESTION

1389. What was in the middle of the wheel that Ezekiel saw in vision? (Ezek. 1:16)

ISRAEL'S SONS SEARCH
Who Are The Players?

Solution on page 266

S	I	M	E	O	N	R	K	W	K	T
X	R	D	J	Z	E	B	U	L	U	N
Z	U	T	B	H	Y	G	K	H	X	I
K	B	M	S	E	D	A	A	D	L	R
Z	E	A	L	T	N	D	D	A	B	J
Q	N	N	E	Y	U	J	T	Y	B	H
M	L	B	V	J	X	H	A	D	L	M
G	R	X	I	N	P	H	M	M	A	X
B	I	S	S	A	C	H	A	R	I	N
N	F	K	N	R	T	Z	P	N	T	N
V	R	R	M	J	O	S	E	P	H	C

- What is the name of the tribe of Israel that begins with the letter "A"? (Gen. 35:26)

- What is the name of the son of Jacob that begins with the letter "S"? (Gen. 35:23)

- What is the name of the tribe of Israel that begins with the letter "B"? (Gen. 35:24)

- What is the name of the son of Jacob that begins with the letter "L"? (Gen. 35:23)

- What is the name of the tribe of Israel that begins with the letter "N"? (Gen. 35:25)

- What is the name of the tribe of Israel that begins with the letter "I"? (Gen. 35:23)

- What is the name of the tribe of Israel that begins with the letter "D"? (Gen. 35:25)

- What is the name of the tribe of Israel that begins with the letter "G"? (Gen. 35:26)

- What is the name of the tribe of Israel that begins with the letter "Z"? (Gen. 35:23)

- What is the name of the tribe of Israel that begins with the letter "J," and whose mother was Leah? (Gen. 29:32, 35)

- What is the name of the tribe in Israel that begins with the letter "R"? (Gen. 29:32)

- What is the name of the tribe in Israel that begins with the letter "J," and whose mother was Rachel? (Gen. 30:22, 24)

52 *Challenged by the Old Testament*

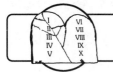
266. God said to Jeremiah that He was a father to Israel. Who does He call His firstborn? (Jer. 31:9)

267. The tent the Israelites worshiped in in the wilderness was called the what? (Ex. 25:9)

268. In what land did the Israelites, as captives, spend four hundred and thirty years? (Ex. 12:40)

269. By whom was Israel's future enslavement in Egypt first prophesied? (Gen. 15:13)

270. In Jeremiah, the Lord said that in the future He would make a new what with Israel? (Jer. 31:31)

271. What did the children of Israel ask Aaron to make when Moses delayed on Sinai? (Ex. 32:1)

272. What was the amount of the atonement money for each male in Israel? (Ex. 30:15)

273. God commanded Ezekiel to cry unto Israel; did He say the house of Israel would harken unto Ezekiel? (Ezek. 3:7)

274. All of Jacob's sons came with him into Egypt, except this one (he was already there). (Ex. 1:1–5)

275. Which three tribes "rose up" out of captivity to go build up the house of the Lord in Jerusalem? (Ezra 1:5)

---

276. How long did Israel mourn for Aaron when he died? (Num. 20:29)

277. God substituted all the males from which tribe of Israel for the firstborn male of each family? (Num. 3:12)

278. What tribes of Israel replaced the tribe of Joseph? (Joshua 14:4)

279. What was set into Aaron's breastplate to represent the tribes of Israel? (Ex. 28:17, 21)

280. Isaiah declared in poetic prophecy that the Lord's people would go into captivity, because they lacked what? (Is. 5:13)

281. Isaiah declares in poetic verse that the Lord's destruction of Israel for its wickedness would have been as Sodom had He not left a very small what? (Is. 1:9)

282. Israel was cursed for taking what "things" from Jericho? (Joshua 7:1)

283. What was marriage outside Israel considered at Ezra's time? (Ezra 9:2, 4)

284. David was given three alternative punishments to chose from for numbering Israel without the Lord commanding it: pestilence, fleeing before enemies, and what else? (2 Sam. 24:13)

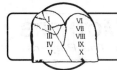
Match the questions on the left with the answers on the right. The solution is on page 270.

A. Simeon was bound and left in Egypt until which of his brothers was brought back to see Joseph? (Gen. 42:24)

B. What material did Pharaoh take away from the Israelites because of Moses, which increased the Israelites labor in making bricks? (Ex. 5:7)

C. The Lord commanded Moses to number the Israelites by their families, every male by his _____. (Num. 1:2)

D. The Israelites wanted Moses to speak with them rather than God, because they feared that if God spoke to them they would what? (Ex. 20:19)

E. The Lord chose the Israelites as His chosen people because of His love for them and His what? (Deut. 7:8)

F. Moses was from what tribe of Israel? (Ex. 2:1)

G. Which of Jacob's sons fathered two tribes? (Joshua 14:4)

H. This name was given to Jacob's son because "a troop cometh." (Gen. 30:11)

I. Caleb was from what tribe in Israel? (Num. 13:6)

J. Oshea (Joshua) was from which tribe of Israel? (Num. 13:8)

K. Which son of Eleazar "stayed" the plague on Israel? (Num. 25:7–8)

Ephraim

Judah

Joseph

Straw

Die

Phinehas

Benjamin

Polls

Oath

Gad

Levi

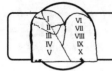

ISRAEL'S MOTHERS
Who Are The Players?

*Match the Sons of Israel in the outer circle with their
mothers in the inner circle. The solution is on page 266*

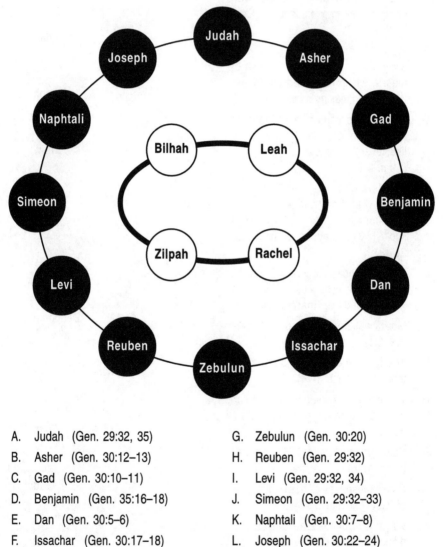

A. Judah (Gen. 29:32, 35)

B. Asher (Gen. 30:12–13)

C. Gad (Gen. 30:10–11)

D. Benjamin (Gen. 35:16–18)

E. Dan (Gen. 30:5–6)

F. Issachar (Gen. 30:17–18)

G. Zebulun (Gen. 30:20)

H. Reuben (Gen. 29:32)

I. Levi (Gen. 29:32, 34)

J. Simeon (Gen. 29:32–33)

K. Naphtali (Gen. 30:7–8)

L. Joseph (Gen. 30:22–24)

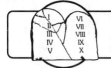
285. What was the price Haman said he would pay to those who had charge of killing the Jews? (Esther 3:9)

286. Zechariah prophesied that Christ would tell the Jews He received his wounds in the what, of his friends? (Zech. 13:6)

287. Why did Jeremiah warn the Jews not to go to Egypt? (Jer. 43:10–11)

288. Mordecai was identified as a "Jew," even though he was from which tribe of Israel? (Esther 2:5)

289. Because of the fear of the Jews, what was the result of Mordecai's order that the Jews could slay all non-Jews? (Esther 8:17)

290. When the Samaritans (adversaries of the Jews) offered, the Jews refused to let them help in building what edifice? (Ezra 4:1–4)

291. Jeremiah prophesied that scattered Israel will gather with Judah out of what land? (Jer. 3:18)

292. Zechariah said God would set everyone against his what? (Zech. 8:10)

293. Who was the king of Persia that fulfilled the prophesy of Jeremiah pertaining to the return of the Jews to Jerusalem? (Ezra 1:1)

294. Why did Zechariah say ten men would take hold of a Jew's skirt? (Zech. 8:23)

295. After discovering the wickedness of Haman, how did the King Ahasuerus counter his order to destroy the Jews? (Esther 8:11)

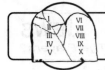

296. Who was Zipporah? (Ex. 2:21)

297. What were the names of Naomi's two daughters-in-law? (Ruth 1:4)

298. What nationality was Micah? (Micah. 1:1)

299. What are the names of the two brothers of Dinah who avenged her defilement? (Gen. 34:25)

300. Who was Huldah? (2 Kings 22:14)

301. What person's bones did Moses take with him at the Exodus? (Ex. 13:19)

302. Who was miraculously provided oil by Elisha to pay her debts? (2 Kings 4:1, 7)

303. Ezekiel prophesied that God would be as a little what, to scattered Israel? (Ezek. 11:16)

304. Who discovered the child Moses floating in a basket in the river? (Ex. 2:5)

305. Who were the three cast into the fiery furnace? (Dan. 3:22–23)

306. Who did Rebekah send Jacob to live with so that he would avoid Esau's anger? (Gen. 27:43)

307. To whom did the Lord send Elijah when the brook Cherith went dry? (1 Kings 17:9)

308. Who became a pillar of salt because she looked back at Sodom and Gomorrah? (Gen. 19:26)

309. Who unrighteously sought the gifts that had been offered to Elisha after Naaman had been healed? (2 Kings 5:21–22)

310. Who told Naaman that he could be healed by a prophet in Israel? (2 Kings 5:2–3)

311. Who told Samuel of Saul's coming? (1 Sam. 9:15–16)

1362. Two men held up Moses' hands to assure Israel's victory over Amalek. One was named Aaron and the other Hur. (Ex. 17:12)

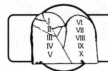

MATCHING IDENTITIES
Who Are The Players?

Match the questions on the left with the answers on the right. The solution is on page 270

A. What was the name of King Ahasuerus' chief prince? (Esther 3:1)

Korah

B. What was the name of Leah's handmaiden? (Gen. 29:24)

Joab

C. What was the name of Phinehas' son? (1 Sam. 4:19, 21)

Jacob

D. Who is the Canaanite captain that was killed by driving a nail through his temples? (Judges 4:22)

Vashti

E. What was the name of the master of Nebuchadnezzar's eunuchs? (Dan. 1:3)

Haman

F. What was the name of Sarah's handmaiden? (Gen. 16:1)

Uriah

G. Who killed Abner? (2 Sam. 3:27)

H. Esau sold his birthright to whom? (Gen. 25:32–33)

Zilpah

I. What was the name of Elisha's servant? (2 Kings 4:8, 12)

Obadiah

J. Who was the first named leader of the two hundred and fifty princes that rebelled against Moses? (Num. 16:1–2)

Ichabod

K. To whom was Hagar a handmaiden? (Gen. 16:1)

Gehazi

L. Which of King Ahasuerus' queens was dethroned? (Esther 1:19)

Sisera

M. What was the name of the servant of Ahab who hid the one hundred prophets? (1 Kings 18:4)

Ashpenaz

N. Who delivered a letter to Joab instructing him to place Uriah in the forefront of the battle so that he would die? (2 Sam. 11:14–15)

Sarai

Hagar

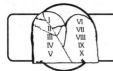
312. Who betrayed Samson's riddle to the Philistines? (Judges 14:16–17)

313. How long did Samson judge Israel? (Judges 15:20)

314. What punishment did the Philistines finally give Samson? (Judges 16:21)

315. When Samson's hair was cut off, how many "locks" were there? (Judges 16:19)

316. How did Samson start the fires that burned the Philistines' corn? (Judges 15:4)

317. Samson used the jawbone of an ass for what purpose? (Judges 15:15)

318. What was Samson's last feat of strength? (Judges 16:29)

319. How did Samson slay one thousand men? (Judges 15:15)

320. What did Samson challenge the Philistines with at his marriage feast? (Judges 14:12)

321. How did the Philistines kill Samson's wife? (Judges 15:6)

322. Who disclosed Samson's strength to the Philistines? (Judges 16:4, 19)

---

323. What nationality was Samson's wife? (Judges 14:1–2)

324. The second lie Samson told Delilah about his strength was that it could be taken away by binding him fast with new what? (Judges 16:11)

325. Samson was from which tribe of Israel? (Judges 13:2, 24)

326. What did the angel say was not to touch the head of Samson? (Judges 13:5)

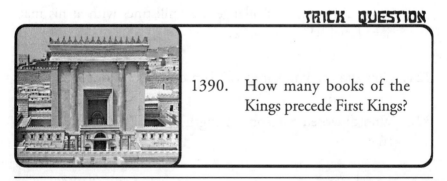

TRICK QUESTION

1390. How many books of the Kings precede First Kings?

SEARCH FOR IDENTITY
Who Are The Players?

Solution on page 278

```
R  N  Z  K  Z  G  R  V  H  T  H  C
J  O  S  H  U  A  O  A  M  A  G  H
N  N  T  D  K  L  I  L  P  Z  H  E
J  Y  V  T  A  D  Z  R  I  P  L  M
E  P  O  N  A  N  O  G  E  A  R  O
N  L  V  B  L  X  I  S  D  J  T  S
O  L  O  E  R  B  O  E  K  O  C  H
C  Y  B  L  Y  J  K  D  L  T  K  M
H  A  R  A  C  H  E  L  L  H  L  Y
B  X  C  Z  D  L  J  L  V  A  F  M
B  I  L  H  A  H  J  M  I  M  M  W
J  C  B  A  T  H  S  H  E  B  A  C
```

- Who fled to Zoar to avoid the destruction of Sodom and Gomorrah? (Gen. 19:22–24)

- Bilhah was the handmaiden to whom? (Gen. 30:1, 4)

- To whom did God reveal Nebuchadnezzar's forgotten dream? (Daniel 2:19)

- Who does it say was three hundred and sixty-five years old when he was taken by God? (Gen. 5:23–24)

- The king over Egypt that enslaved the Israelites was noted as one who knew not whom? (Ex. 1:8)

- What was the name of Rachel's handmaiden? (Gen. 30:4)

- What was the name of the champion of the Philistines who challenged Israel? (1 Sam. 17:4)

- What was the name of the false god that was called the abomination of Moab? (1 Kings 11:7)

- Which of Naomi's daughters-in-law left her? (Ruth 1:14–15)

- "As I was with Moses, so I will be with thee." Who is the "thee" the scripture refers to? (Joshua 1:1, 5)

- What is the name of the priest who saw Hannah praying before the Lord? (1 Sam. 1:12)

- Who went to King David and reminded him that he had promised that her son would be the next king? (1 Kings 1:15–17)

- What was the name of the only brother Abimelech did not kill? (Judges 9:5)

- What name did the Lord give the place where he confounded the language of the people? (Gen. 11:9)

- Which of Ahab's servants was told to tell Ahab that Elijah was coming? (1 Kings 18:7, 11)

Challenged by the Old Testament 63

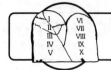
327. When Esther came before the king improperly, she must die unless he held out to her his golden what? (Esther 4:11)

328. What request did Esther make of the king at her second banquet? (Esther 7:3)

329. What is the name of the person that raised Esther? (Esther 2:5, 7)

330. Who did Esther invite to her banquets with the king? (Esther 5:4, 8)

331. What did Esther request of her people in her behalf for three days and nights? (Esther 4:16)

332. What was the risk Esther took by going before the king without first being summoned? (Esther 4:11)

333. Esther, when she went before King Ahasuerus, requested that he and Haman come to her what? (Esther 5:4)

334. What did Haman request of Esther after she gave her second banquet? (Esther 7:7)

335. What did Esther request of the king at her first banquet? (Esther 5:8)

336. What plot did Mordecai uncover? (Esther 2: 21, 22)

337. What did Mordecai rend when he heard of Haman's order? (Esther 4:1)

338. What made Haman angry at Mordecai? (Esther 3:2)

339. Who did Haman believe was to receive the king's honor? (Esther 6:6)

340. What did Mordecai ask Esther to do that could cause her to risk her life? (Esther 4:8)

341. What did Esther not declare to king Ahasuerus, when she became queen? (Esther 2:10)

342. What order involving Esther and her kin could king Ahasuerus not reverse once it was sealed with his ring? (Esther 3:13; 8:8)

343. What structure did Haman prepare for Mordecai? (Esther 5:14)

344. Because Esther so pleased the king, what did he offer her? (Esther 5:3)

345. What was Esther's other name? (Esther 2:7)

346. Who did Esther designate as the wicked enemy of her people? (Esther 7:6)

347. Esther's last request of King Ahasuerus was that he hang how many of Haman's sons? (Esther 9:13)

348. When Esther went before King Ahasueras, she requested that the king and who, come to her banquet? (Esther 5:4)

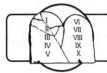

DAVID AND BATHSHEBA
Who Are The Players?

Solution on page 261

Across

2 What was David's sin with Bathsheba? (2 Sam. 11:4)

3 David declared to Goliath that he would defeat him so that all the world would know that this Deity was with Israel. (1 Sam. 17:46)

5 Prior to Goliath, David had evidenced his bravery by killing a lion and a what? (1 Sam 17:36)

8 To prove that he was loyal to Saul, David cut off the skirt of Saul's what, while he slept? (1 Sam. 24:4)

9 David ordered Uriah to the front of the battle so that he would be smitten and do what? (2 Sam. 11:15)

10 David killed Goliath by cutting his _____ off. (1 Sam. 17:51)

13 David took three things with him to fight Goliath, his staff, five stones, and his what? (1 Sam. 17:40)

15 Was Solomon Bathsheba's first or second son? (2 Sam. 12:24)

17 David fasted and wept for the first child he had with Bathsheba only when it was in what condition? (2 Sam. 12:15–16, 19–20)

19 Who did David send for after he discovered Bathsheba's pregnancy? (2 Sam. 11:6)

22 David rejected wearing Saul's armor to fight Goliath because it had not been what? (1 Sam. 17:39)

23 When David volunteered to fight Goliath, Saul told David that he was not able to go against him because he was but a what? (1 Sam. 17:33)

24 Michal despised David because of his public what? (2 Sam. 6:16)

25 How old was David when he became king over all Israel? (2 Sam. 5:4)

Down

1 Nathan delivered a parable to David concerning his sin. Bathsheba was represented in the parable as a little ewe what? (2 Sam. 12:3)

4 The fate of Bathsheba's first child with David was that it what? (2 Sam. 12:19)

6 David was given three alternative punishments to choose from for numbering Israel without the Lord commanding it: Famine, fleeing from what adversaries, and pestilence? (2 Sam. 24:13)

7 After their affair, Bathsheba an-nounced to David that she was with what? (2 Sam. 11:5)

9 When Goliath first saw David, he declared, "Am I a _____ ?" (1 Sam. 17:43)

11 When David said he would go and fight Goliath, Saul gave David his what? (1 Sam. 17:38)

12 When David first saw Bathsheba, what was she doing? (2 Sam. 11:2)

14 David was on this part of his palace when he first saw Bathsheba. (2 Sam. 11:2)

16 When Samuel reviewed the sons of Jesse, what was David tending? (1 Sam. 16:11)

18 The Amalekite who killed Saul brought Saul's bracelet and his _____ to David. (2 Sam. 1:10)

20 What prophet told Bathsheba to go to David for Solomon's sake? (1 Kings 1:11–13)

21 David was first made king over which tribe in Israel? (2 Sam. 2:4)

TRUE OR FALSE

1363. Moses, because of the order of Pharaoh to kill all male infants, was placed in the "flags by the river's brink" in an ark made of bulrushes. (Ex. 2:3)

Ezekiel was an amazing prophet. The scriptures indicate that he was privileged to see vision after vision. In one of his greatest visions he saw a large valley "full of bones." He observed that the bones were "very dry," and indicated that they had been in that condition for some time. Then the Lord began asking Ezekiel questions about the bones.

"Can these bones live?" the Lord asked.

Ezekiel, perhaps a little fearful of what the Lord would do, responded, "O Lord GOD, thou knowest."

Then the Lord said to Ezekiel, "Prophesy upon these bones and say unto them, O ye dry bones, hear the word of the Lord." (Almost everyone has heard the famous old spiritual song, *Dem Bones*. It is based on this great vision.)

So Ezekiel prophesied, and it reports that there "was a noise, and behold a shaking, and the bones came together, bone to his bone." (You can almost hear the music as you read the story!)

Then the scripture reports that sinews and flesh came upon the bones and skin covered them, "but there was no breath in them." So the Lord commanded Ezekiel to again prophesy and say to the wind, "Thus saith the Lord GOD; Come from the four winds, O breath, and breathe upon these slain." And so Ezekiel prophesied, " and the breath came into them, and they lived, and stood up upon their feet, an exceeding great army."

We are not told what happened to the army, but we are told what the vision represents.

1411. What did the dry bones that Ezekiel saw raised to an exceeding great army represent? (Ezek. 37:11)

Family Relations

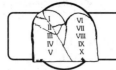

349. From what tribe in Israel was Jeroboam a descendant? (1 Kings 11:26)

350. Which of Abraham's brothers died before their father? (Gen. 11:28)

351. Who did Jacob send messengers and gifts to before meeting with him because he feared him? (Gen. 32:6–21)

352. Which of David's sons killed his brother Amnon for defiling his sister? (2 Sam. 13:28–29)

353. What was the name of the nephew that Abraham took with him to the land of Canaan? (Gen. 12:5)

354. Kish was the father of which king of Israel? (1 Sam. 9:1–2)

355. How does the Bible explain the fact that Sarah was Abraham's sister? (Gen. 20:12)

356. Who was the prophetess that was also Aaron's sister? (Ex. 15:20)

357. What relation was Nadab and Abihu to Aaron? (Ex. 28:1)

358. Phinehas (the priest) was the son of whom? (Num. 25:7)

359. What family relations did Lot leave behind in Sodom and Gomorrah? (Gen. 19:14)

360. What happened to Naomi's sons in Moab? (Ruth 1:5)

361. What was the relationship of Eliezer to Moses? (Ex. 18:2–4)

362. What was the name of Rachel's sister? (Gen. 29:16)

363. What was the name of Judah's firstborn who was slain by the Lord? (Gen. 38:7)

364. What relation was Aaron to Moses? (Ex. 4:14)

365. What is the name of Absalom's sister (who was defiled by Amnon)? (2 Sam. 13:1)

366. What was the name of Saul's oldest son? (1 Sam. 14:1)

367. How many daughters-in-law did Naomi have? (Ruth 1:4)

368. What was the name of the daughter-in-law that bore Judah children? (Gen. 38:24)

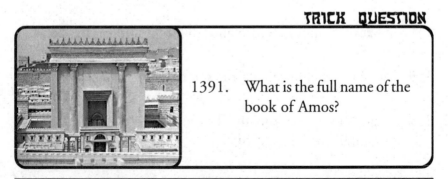

TRICK QUESTION

1391. What is the full name of the book of Amos?

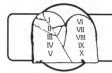

HUSBANDS AND WIVES
Family Relations

*Match the questions on the left with the answers on the
right. The solution is on page 264*

A. Who was Abigail's first husband? (1 Sam. 25:14)

B. Who was David's third wife? (1 Sam. 25:43)

C. Who was Uriah the Hittite's wife? (2 Sam. 11:3)

D. Who was Rebekah's husband? (Gen. 24:67)

E. What was the name of Jacob's first wife? (Gen. 29:23)

F. Which of Elkanah's wives had no children? (1 Sam. 1:2)

G. Who was Elisheba's husband? (Ex. 6:23)

H. What was the name of David's first wife? (1 Sam. 18:27)

I. What was the name of Moses' wife? (Ex. 2:21)

J. What was the name of Joseph's wife? (Gen. 41:45)

K. What was the name of the wife of Haman? (Esther 6:13)

L. Who was Ruth's first husband? (Ruth 4:10)

M. Who was David's second wife? (1 Sam. 25:42)

N. To whom was Hagar given as a wife? (Gen. 16:3)

Mahlon

Zipporah

Leah

Michal

Zeresh

Ahinoam

Abraham

Nabal

Abigail

Hannah

Isaac

Bathsheba

Asenath

Aaron

Challenged by the Old Testament

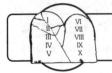

Solution on page 262

Across

4   Which of David's sons rebelled against him and attempted to make himself king over Israel? (2 Sam. 15:10)

7   Which of Benjamin's brothers pledged himself as surety for Benjamin's safe journey into Egypt? (Gen. 43:8–9)

9   What combination of children did Rebekah bear at her first childbirth? (Gen. 25:23)

11 What was the name of Ruth's child? (Ruth 4:17)

13 What was the name of Judah's second born who was slain by the Lord? (Gen. 38:9–10)

14 Did Rebekah love her son Esau or her son Jacob? (Gen. 25:28)

16 Who was the brother of Shem and Ham? (Gen. 5:32)

18 Who was the brother of Shem and Japheth? (Gen. 5:32)

19 From which son of Noah did Abraham descend? (Gen. 11:10–27)

21 What was the name of Cain's first brother? (Gen. 4:2)

23 What was the name of Moses' first son? (Ex. 2:22)

24 The Lord declared that His people were foolish, had not known Him, and were what kind of children? (Jer. 4:22)

25 Queen Athaliah massacred all but one of these relatives. (2 Kings 11:1–2)

Down

1 Hannah vowed that if the Lord would give her a son, this instrument would never come upon the child's head. (1 Sam. 1:11)

2 According to Genesis, did Isaac love Esau or Jacob? (Gen. 25:28)

3 The birthright of Israel went to the lineage of which son? (1 Chron. 5:1)

5 This Moabitess was one of Jesus' ancestors. (Ruth 1:4; 4:17)

6 What was the name of Adam's first son? (Gen. 4:1)

8 What was the name of the daughter of Leah? (Gen. 30:21)

10 What righteous son of Adam and Eve replaced Abel? (Gen. 4:25)

12 What was the relationship between Nahor and Abram? (Gen. 11:27)

15 In Jeremiah, the Lord warned the children of which tribe of Israel to flee Jerusalem before its destruction? (Jer. 6:1)

17 What queen massacred her grand-children? (2 Kings 11:1–2)

19 What is the relationship of Miriam to Aaron? (Ex. 15:20)

20 What was the name of Jacob's first-born? (Gen. 29:32)

22 How many children did Hosea have? (Hosea 1:3, 6–8)

TRUE OR FALSE

1364. Elijah poured water on his sacrifice five times during his contest with the priests of Baal. (1 Kings 18:34)

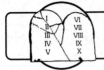
369. Job said to his wife: "What? Shall we receive good at the hand of God, and shall we not receive _____?" (Job 2:10)

370. How many wives did Solomon have? (1 Kings 11:3)

371. Who smote Nabal, Abigail's first husband? (1 Sam. 25:38)

372. What did Job's wife tell him to do? (Job 2:9)

373. What are the names of Jacob's four wives? (Gen. 35:23–26)

374. Abraham married what family relation? (Gen. 20:12)

375. Who gave Hagar to Abraham as a wife? (Gen. 16:3)

376. How many years did Jacob serve Laban in order to secure Rachel as his wife? (Gen. 29:27)

377. The name of Samson's wife is unknown, but she lived where in Philstia? (Judges 14:1)

378. What was the name of Isaac's wife? (Gen. 24:51)

379. What happen to Naomi's husband in Moab? (Ruth 1:3)

380. What name did Adam give his wife? (Gen. 3:20)

381. In Genesis, who does it say the sons of God took to wife? (Gen. 6:2)

382. When a man took a new wife, how long was he free from war and business obligations and able to remain at home? (Deut. 24:5)

383. What was the name of Aaron's wife? (Ex. 6:23)

384. What happened to Lot's wife when she looked back at the destruction of Sodom and Gomorrah? (Gen. 19:26)

385. What did Jacob agree to pay for Rachel so that she could be his wife? (Gen. 29:18)

386. Who was Bathsheba's first husband? (2 Sam. 11:3)

387. What was the name of Naomi's husband? (Ruth 1:2)

388. What was the name of the woman Abraham took to wife after Sarah died? (Gen. 25:1)

389. How many children did Michal, David's first wife, have? (2 Sam. 6:23)

390. Who were Elkanah's two wives? (1 Sam. 1:2)

391. What was the name of Jacob's second wife? (Gen. 29:28)

SEARCHING FOR FATHERS

Family Relations

Solution on page 279

```
G  H  V  Q  K  H  H  I  L  K  I  A  H  N
L  N  X  R  C  B  A  K  G  H  V  X  R  E
P  T  G  E  N  E  K  M  A  Y  L  O  T  B
Q  Y  M  Q  D  T  X  O  I  B  M  X  V  U
T  A  K  R  T  H  N  P  F  T  H  M  M  C
L  W  M  H  N  U  C  K  M  A  T  D  M  H
N  B  R  H  G  E  P  L  I  P  M  A  Z  A
E  W  J  F  K  L  N  H  J  F  X  Z  I  D
L  D  R  O  R  R  C  M  N  O  A  H  Q  N
K  R  Z  J  S  E  A  B  I  H  A  I  L  E
A  Y  M  T  R  E  R  F  M  M  V  N  H  Z
N  P  T  E  P  K  P  T  K  N  O  M  Z  Z
A  T  B  H  R  K  Y  H  C  Z  R  A  K  A
H  A  H  A  S  U  E  R  U  S  L  G  B  R
```

- Who was Noah's father? (Gen. 5:28–29)

- Who was Japheth's father? (Gen. 5:32)

- Who was King Belshazzar's father? (Dan. 5:2)

- Who was Ephraim's father? (Gen. 41:51–52)

- Who was the father of Zechariah? (Zech. 1:1)

- Who fathered the Moabites? (Gen. 19:36–37)

- Find the father of Lot's daughters' children. (Gen. 19:36)

- Find the name of Rachel's father. (Gen. 24:24)

- Who was Ham's father? (Gen. 5:32)

- Who was the father of Darius? (Dan. 9:1)

- What was the name of Jonah's father? (Jonah 1:1)

- Who was Samuel's father? (1 Sam. 1:19–20)

- Who was Jeremiah's father? (Jer. 1:1)

- Who was the father of Esther? (Esther 2:15)

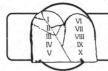

ALL ABOUT MOTHERS
Family Relations

Match the questions on the left with the answers on the right. The solution is on page 257

A. To determine which harlot was the mother, what did Solomon propose to do with a baby? (1 Kings 3:25)

A daughter

B. Who was Dinah's mother? (Gen. 30:20–21)

An angel

C. What was the name of Ruth's mother-in-law? (Ruth 1:2)

Divide it in half

D. What relation was Benammi's mother to Lot? (Gen. 19:36, 38)

Unknown

E. Who was Ishmael's mother? (Gen. 16:8, 11)

Naomi

F. Who was Isaac's mother? (Gen. 17:19)

Leah

G. What was Samson's mother's name? (Judges 13:3)

Hagar

H. Who told the future mother of Samson that she would give birth? (Judges 13:3)

Sarah

392. Who grabbed his brother's heel at birth? (Gen. 25:26)

393. What were the names of Naomi's two sons? (Ruth 1:2)

394. What was the name of Isaac's firstborn? (Gen. 25:25)

395. What are the names of Eli's two sons who died by the hand of the Lord? (1 Sam. 2:34)

396. What is the name of the son of Isaiah who went with Isaiah to meet Ahaz? (Is. 7:3)

397. What relation was Rebekah's grandfather to Abraham? (Gen. 24:15)

398. Who did Abraham tell Sarah to tell the Egyptians she was? (Gen. 12:13)

399. What were the names of Aaron's two sons whom the Lord devoured with fire for disobeying Him? (Lev. 10:1–2)

400. What was the name of Sarah's only son? (Gen. 17:19)

401. What family relationship did Ezekiel use when comparing Israel with Judah? (Ezek. 23:2)

402. How did the little children mock Elisha? (2 Kings 2:23)

403. When Elisha raised a dead child, what was the first thing the child did? (2 Kings 4:35)

404. What were the names of Samuel's two sons? (1 Sam. 8:2)

405. Who was known as the beautiful son of David? (2 Sam. 14:25)

406. Although Michal had no children of her own, whose children did she raise? (1 Sam. 18:19; 2 Sam. 21:8)

TRICK QUESTION

1392. At the age of twenty, males of each tribe of Jacob were considered ready to go to war. What was the age of males in Israel when they could go to war? (Num. 1:20)

BROTHERS AND RELATIVES
Family Relations

Solution on page 259

```
N  L  Z  L  Z  L  A  B  A  N  H  J  R  Z  W
Z  E  Z  Z  T  H  B  R  B  R  M  R  G  A  L
S  I  S  T  E  R  I  N  L  A  W  C  L  K  R
J  C  H  A  P  N  A  H  O  R  Z  N  T  L  M
H  S  M  L  U  V  R  B  J  S  I  S  T  E  R
A  F  O  H  W  E  N  Y  Z  R  P  H  K  M  K
L  M  M  N  H  I  P  N  E  B  K  D  B  J  X
F  M  P  T  S  K  N  T  B  N  Y  N  R  N  T
S  T  A  U  H  I  H  E  K  N  I  S  O  T  Y
I  F  O  J  R  G  N  W  P  M  N  O  T  K  T
S  C  L  Y  U  J  M  L  A  H  T  N  H  K  K
T  T  J  A  L  S  C  J  A  W  E  C  E  L  F
E  K  D  K  J  H  N  H  L  W  I  W  R  Y  B
R  W  L  T  R  E  L  M  Y  R  D  F  R  N  M
G  F  M  L  B  M  T  M  Q  Z  N  X  E  M  K
```

- What relation was Tamar to Judah? (Gen. 38:24)

- What was the name of Rebekah's brother? (Gen. 24:29)

- The Edomites were descendants from what brother of Jacob? (Ob. 1:6–10)

- Moses told Pharaoh that God said to let his _____ (relative) go, or He would slay Pharaoh's son, even his firstborn. (Ex. 4:23)

- What relation was Abner to Saul? (1 Sam. 14:50)

- Abraham's two brothers were named Haran and what? (Gen. 11:27)

- Lot could NOT convince what male relatives to leave Sodom? (Gen. 19:14)

- Who was the brother of Ham and Japheth? (Gen. 5:32)

- God declared to Jeremiah that He was what relation to Israel? (Jer. 31:9)

- Abraham told Abimelech that Sarah was not his wife, but his what? (Gen. 20:2)

- What was Jacob's relationship to Rachel's father? (Gen. 29:13)

- When Jacob meets Rachel, he tells her that he is her father's what? (Gen. 29:12–13)

- Judah was pledged as surety for which brother's safe return from Egypt? (Gen. 42:36; 43:8–9)

- What relation was Orpah to Ruth? (Ruth 1:3–4)

- Lot fled from Sodom before its destruction. He took his _____ and his two daughters with him. (Gen. 19:15)

- Sarah had the same father as Abraham, but not the same mother; therefore, what relation was she to Abraham? (Gen. 20:12)

TRUE OR FALSE

1365. After being conquered by the King of Babylon, the Lord told the remnant of Judah NOT to go to Egypt. (Jer. 42:19)

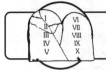

FATHERS CROSSWORD
Family Relations

Solution on page 263

Across

2 Who was the father of Samson? (Judges 13:2)

5 Who was Gershom's father? (Ex. 2:21–22)

6 Who was Shem's father? (Gen. 5:32)

9 Who was the father of Cain? (Gen. 4:1)

10 Who was the father of Solomon? (2 Sam. 12:24)

12 Who was the murderer father of Enoch that lived in Nod? (Gen. 4:17)

14 Who was Methuselah's father? (Gen. 5:21)

17 Who fathered the children of Ammon? (Gen. 19:36–38)

18 Who was David's great-grandfather? (Ruth 4:21–22)

19 Who was the father of the prophet Joel? (Joel 1:1)

22 Who was Hezekiah's father? (2 Kings 18:1)

23 Who was Nadab's father? (Ex. 6:23)

25 Who was Michal's (David's first wife) father? (1 Sam. 18:27)

26 Who was the father of Jacob? (Gen. 25:21, 26)

27 Who was the father of Canaan? (Gen. 9:18)

28 Who was Manasseh's father? (Gen. 41:51)

Down

1 Who is the father of Hosea? (Hosea 1:1)

3 Who was Isaiah's father? (Is. 1:1)

4 Who was Abraham's father? (Gen. 11:27)

7 Who was Lot's father? (Gen. 11:31)

8 Who was the father of Joel and Abiah? (1 Sam. 8:2)

11 Who was Jeroboam's father? (1 Kings 11:26)

13 Who was the father of Isaac? (Gen. 21:3)

15 Who was the father of Zephaniah? (Zeph. 1:1)

16 Who was the father of Samuel? (1 Sam. 1:19–20)

18 Who was Ezekiel's father? (Ezek. 1:3)

20 Who was the father of the Edomites? (Gen. 36:43)

21 What was the name of Rachel's father? (Gen. 29:5–6)

24 Who was Saul's father? (1 Sam. 9:1–2)

TRICK QUESTION

1393. David divided the work of the santuary into twenty-four courses, how many "courses" did David divide the sons of Levi into to do its work? (1 Chron. 24:17–19)

Like the Jews of old, I love Elijah. But the people of Israel were very wicked during his day—to the point that he claimed, "I, even I only, remain a prophet of the Lord." He said this while comparing himself to the four hundred and fifty false prophets of the god that the people were worshiping at the time. One day Elijah decided to propose a contest with these false prophets. He would prepare a sacrifice to his God, and the false prophets would prepare one to their god. Then they would call upon their respective gods to send down fire to consume the sacrifices. And so, as the people watched, the contest began.

When their sacrifice was ready, the false prophets called to their god to send down fire and consume it—but nothing happened. Elijah observed their antics throughout the day, and finally he mocked the false prophets saying, "Cry aloud: for he is a god; either he is talking, or he is pursuing, or he is in a journey, or peradventure he sleepeth, and must be awakened."

The false prophets worked all the harder, even cutting themselves with knives and lancets as was their custom, until their blood gushed out upon them. But no fire came.

Finally, Elijah repaired an altar of the Lord that had been broken down. He positioned twelve rocks at its base to represent the tribes of Israel. He made a trench around it and placed wood upon it, and on the wood he placed the sacrifice. Then he poured four barrels of water all over the sacrifice and the wood. He did this three times, until the water "ran round about the altar" and filled the trench. Then he called upon the Lord.

Immediately, fire came from the Lord "and consumed the burnt sacrifice, and the wood, and the stones, and the dust, and licked up the water that was in the trench." Elijah had proved his God was true, and the frightened people fell upon their faces crying, "The Lord, he is the God; the Lord, he is the God."

And that leads us to the question:

1412.   In Elijah's contest with the four hundred and fifty false prophets, who was the false god that the prophets pled with to consume their sacrifice? (1 Kings 18:21)

Moses, Moses, Moses!

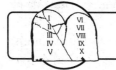

V

407. Because Aaron could speak well, God said that he would become Moses' what? (Ex. 4:16)

408. When Aaron was called to assist Moses, Moses would be as what Deity to Aaron? (Ex. 4:16)

409. How old was Moses when he first went to see Pharaoh? (Ex. 7:7)

410. How long did Moses remain with God waiting for the second set of tablets? (Ex. 34:28)

411. Moses instructed the Israelites that they were neither to diminish nor to what, to the things he had commanded them? (Deut. 12:32)

412. The Lord often speaks to prophets in dreams, but how did He speak to Moses? (Num. 12:6, 8)

413. What was the relationship of Jethro to Moses? (Ex. 3:1)

414. When Moses was born, what edict of Pharaoh's did he fall under? (Ex. 1:16)

415. After the death of Moses, who said he would be with Joshua? (Joshua 1:1, 5)

416. What was the name of Moses' second son? (Ex. 18:2–4)

417. Who does it say met Moses by the way in the inn and sought to kill him as he returned to Egypt from Midian? (Ex. 4:24)

418. What did Moses do when the Lord told him to cast his rod upon the ground, and it turned into a serpent? (Ex. 4:3)

419. The infant Moses floated in the river in an ark made of what? (Ex. 2:3)

420. Who watched the baby Moses while he was in the basket on the river? (Ex. 2:4)

421. How much older was Aaron than Moses? (Ex. 7:7)

422. What quality did Moses possess above all other men on earth? (Num. 12:3)

423. God made Moses as what deity to Pharaoh? (Ex. 7:1)

424. Who did Moses kill and bury in the sand, an act that forced him to leave Egypt? (Ex. 2:12)

425. Moses complained to the Lord at his call because he was not _____, but slow of speech and tongue. (Ex. 4:10)

426. Who appeared to Moses in the burning bush? (Ex. 3:2)

427. What did Moses wish all the Lord's people were? (Num. 11:29)

428. The Lord said to Moses, "and thou shalt be to him instead of God." To whom was the Lord referring? (Ex. 4:14–16)

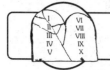

429. Did the first plagues Moses caused to come upon Egypt (prior to the plague of flies) also affect Israel? (Ex. 8:22)

430. Did Pharaoh's magicians produce frogs during Moses' plagues? (Ex. 8:7)

431. Did Moses bring a plague of locusts upon Egypt? (Ex. 10:13–14)

432. Did Pharaoh's magicians turn water into blood? (Ex. 7:22)

433. Pharaoh was to see the face of Moses no more after which plague? (Ex. 10:22, 28)

434. Which of Moses' plagues upon Egypt came up out of the river? (Ex. 8:3)

435. What effect did Moses' plague have on Egyptian cattle? (Ex. 9:6)

436. What ran along the ground when Moses brought the plague of hail upon the Egyptians? (Ex. 9:23)

437. How long did the river remain blood when Moses cursed it before Pharaoh? (Ex. 7:25)

438. How long did the plague of darkness last that Moses brought upon Egypt? (Ex. 10:22)

439. Did Pharaoh's magicians produce lice during the plagues of Moses? (Ex. 8:18)

440. At which of Moses' plagues did Pharaoh first say he would let Israel go? (Ex. 8:8)

441. What was Moses' last plague upon Egypt before the death of the firstborn? (Ex. 10:22)

442. What was the first of Moses' plagues that Pharaoh's magicians could not duplicate? (Ex. 8:18)

443. What was the last plague inflicted upon Egypt before Pharaoh would let the Israelite people go? (Ex. 11:5)

444. Which of Moses' plagues upon Egypt became fire that ran along the ground? (Ex. 9:23)

445. Which of Moses' plagues was the first to only affect the Egyptians? (Ex. 8:21–22)

446. What plague upon Egypt ate the remainder of the crops that the hail did not destroy? (Ex. 10:12)

447. How did Phinehas "stay the plague" from the children of Israel? (Num. 25:8)

448. When Moses sprinkled ashes toward heaven, what broke forth with blains upon all men and beasts throughout Egypt? (Ex. 9:9)

449. What happened when Aaron struck the dust of the land before Pharaoh? (Ex. 8:16)

450. Which of the plagues that Moses brought upon Egypt lasted three days? (Ex. 10:22)

TEN COMMANDMENTS MATCH
Moses, Moses, Moses!

Match the questions on the left with the answers on the right. The solution is on page 282

A. Which commandment prohibits the taking of God's name in vain? (Ex. 20:1–17 (7))

Five

B. Which commandment prohibits adultery? (Ex. 20:1–17 (14))

Eight

C. Which commandment prohibits coveting? (Ex. 20:1–17 (17))

Three

D. Which commandment prohibits having other gods before God the Father? (Ex. 1–17 (3))

Ten

E. Which commandment requires us to honor our father and mother? (Ex. 1–17 (12))

Four

F. Which commandment prohibits graven images? (Ex. 1–17 (4))

Seven

G. Which commandment prohibits the bearing of false witness? (Ex. 1–17 (16))

One

H. Which commandment requires us to keep the Sabbath day holy? (Ex. 1–17 (8))

Nine

I. Which commandment prohibits stealing? (Ex. 1–17 (15))

Two

J. Which commandment prohibits killing? (Ex. 1–17 (13))

Six

IMAGERY WORD SEARCH

Moses, Moses, Moses!

Solution on page 265

S	W	I	N	D	C	S	Y	M	X	G	K
M	W	B	A	M	H	R	H	F	C	R	R
O	I	A	M	P	I	E	N	O	A	C	T
O	N	B	P	A	P	S	A	B	N	S	P
T	D	E	H	F	S	A	D	R	E	E	W
H	O	S	E	A	B	O	R	L	T	G	E
N	W	Z	C	L	O	A	G	E	R	V	A
D	S	R	R	L	I	A	Y	F	L	R	R
T	A	W	B	B	E	J	F	I	R	E	Y
C	Z	E	R	U	B	B	A	B	E	L	C
X	P	A	S	T	O	R	S	H	M	B	W
T	R	I	G	H	T	K	L	N	N	K	V

- Isaiah said that we should wait upon the Lord, and mount up with wings, like what regal birds? (Is. 40:31)

- Speaking through Haggai the prophet, who did the Lord say he would make "as a signet"? (Haggai 2:23)

- To Zephaniah, the Lord said that the day would come when he would punish all who were clothed with strange what? (Zeph. 1:8)

- Speaking of the last days in poetic imagery, Isaiah says the Lord will give children to be princes, and _____ will rule over Judah. (Is. 3:4)

- In Samson's riddle, a beehive filled with honey was housed inside a lion's what (modern spelling)? (Judges 14:8)

- Jeremiah said "woe" to what leaders who scattered the sheep of the Lord? (Jer. 23:1)

- The Lord told Samuel that men look on the outward appearance, but the Lord looks on the what? (1 Sam. 16:7)

- Isaiah said they that wait upon the Lord will run and not be what? (Isa 40:31)

- What did Moses put on Aaron's ear, thumb, and big toe to consecrate him? (Lev. 8:23)

- Elijah was commanded to stand on the mount before the Lord, but when the Lord passed by, he was not in the wind, in the earthquake, nor in this element. (1 Kings 19:11–12)

- When Moses came down from Sinai, he put a veil upon his face because it _____. (Ex. 34:35)

- What part of heaven will open if we pay our tithes and offerings? (Mal. 3:10)

- According to Isaiah, which of God's hands "spanned the heavens"? (Is. 48:13)

- Isaiah declared in poetic verse that Israel's watchmen were dumb dogs that cannot do what? (Is. 56:10)

- Esau was called an hairy man; what kind of man was Jacob? (Gen. 27:11)

- What prophet was described as "an hairy man"? (2 Kings 1:8)

- Jacob was called a smooth man, what kind of man was Esau called? (Gen. 27:11)

- Elijah was commanded to stand on the mount before the Lord, but as the Lord passed by, he was not in the fire, the earthquake, nor the what? (1 Kings 19:11–12)

- In the vision of Zechariah, what was the color of the horses in the fourth chariot? (Zech. 6:3)

TRUE OR FALSE

1366. Naaman, the commander of Syria's host, had leprosy. (2 Kings 5:1)

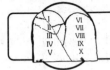

451. By day, the Lord sent what vaporous pillar before the Israelites to guide them after the Exodus? (Ex. 13:21)

452. How did Israel pass through the sea at the Exodus? (Ex. 14:16)

453. After the Exodus, the firstborn of man and beast of Israel was dedicated to whom? (Ex. 13:1–2)

454. How long had the Israelites sojourned in Egypt before the Exodus occurred? (Ex. 12:40)

455. Name one of the three purposes God said He had for having the children of Israel wander forty years in the wilderness. (Deut. 8:16)

456. What told the Israelites when to travel during their journey in the wilderness? (Num. 9:17)

457. What did the Lord require to be sanctified to Him of both children and beast after the Exodus? (Ex. 13:2)

458. What did the Lord send before the Exodus camp of Israel by night? (Ex. 13:21)

459. When Israel left Egypt, how did they "spoil" the Egyptians? (Ex. 12:35–36)

460. What did God say he would send from Sinai to lead the Israelites in the wilderness? (Ex. 23:20)

461. What did it take all night to "divide" during the Exodus? (Ex. 14:21)

462. What happened to the Israelites' clothing while they wandered forty years in the wilderness? (Deut. 8:4)

463. Who did Moses take with him to worship God on Sinai during the Exodus? (Ex. 24:1)

464. What was lacking at Israel's camp at Rephidion? (Ex. 17:1)

465. What sound gave notice for the Israelites to assemble at the tabernacle during the journey in the wilderness? (Num. 10:2)

466. What was Israel's punishment for not entering the promised land at the time of the Exodus? (Num. 14:33)

467. What did Nehemiah say the Israelites lacked during their journey in the wilderness? (Neh. 9:21)

468. What did the whole congregation of Israel do against Moses and Aaron in the wilderness? (Ex. 16:2)

469. Approximately how many men left Egypt at the Exodus? (Ex. 12:37)

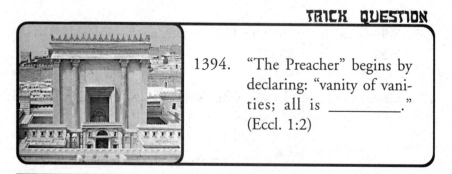

TRICK QUESTION

1394. "The Preacher" begins by declaring: "vanity of vanities; all is _____." (Eccl. 1:2)

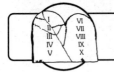

470. Before partaking of the forbidden fruit, how were Adam and Eve dressed in Eden? (Gen. 2:25)

471. What Levitical sin was cleansed by Nehemiah? (Neh. 13:29–30)

472. In Jeremiah, God declared that He was weary with what? (Jer. 15:6)

473. What sin was Ezra most concerned about? (Ezra 9:2)

474. How did the "scapegoat" receive Israel's sins? (Lev. 16:21)

475. What King was given a choice by God between three punishments for his sins? (2 Sam. 24:13)

476. Who had robbed God of His tithes and offerings according to Malachi? (Mal. 3:8)

477. Solomon violated God's commandments because his wives turned him to other what? (1 Kings 11:4)

478. What did man rob from God according to Malachi? (Mal. 3:8)

479. Under the Law of Moses, what was given Israel's sins each year by the laying on of hands? (Lev. 16:8, 21)

480. What great sin did Abimelech commit? (Judges 9:5)

481. How many "woes" did Habakkuk recite against the wicked? (Hab. 2)

482. Jeremiah said Judah's sin was so great that it kindled a _____ in God's anger. (Jer. 17:4)

483. What did Rachel steal from her father when she left with Jacob? (Gen. 31:30, 34)

484. Who killed Abel? (Gen. 4:8)

485. How many days did Ezekiel lay on his right side as a sign to Judah of their sins? (Ezek. 4:6)

486. Who was the first to partake of the forbidden fruit? (Gen. 3:6)

487. Among other sins, Amos said Israel had sinned against the _____, who are always with us. (Amos 2:6–7)

488. After his transgression, Adam could not eat of what tree? (Gen. 3:22–23)

489. According to Isaiah, in order to loose the bands of wickedness we should do what? (Is. 58:6)

490. In Jeremiah, the Lord declared that the people sinned after every _____ of their evil hearts. (Jer. 16:12)

491. What was the only recorded sin that was accounted to David? (1 Kings 15:5)

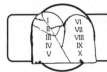
492. What chapter in Leviticus records the blessings and cursings for obedience or disobedience in the Law of Moses?

493. When a man found an uncleanliness in his wife, according to the Law of Moses he could write her a what? (Deut. 24:1)

494. What was the box that contained the tablets of the Law called? (Ex. 25:10; Num. 10:33)

495. Were the Israelites to sanctify themselves holy before the Lord under the Law of Moses? (Lev. 11:44)

496. What was the punishment for a stubborn and rebellious son under the Law of Moses? (Deut. 21:18, 21)

497. Who could not reach a slayer who killed any person unawares when he was in a city of refuge? (Joshua 20:4–5)

498. What *Old Testament* book describes the offerings, sacrifices, and rules of the Law of Moses?

499. When were the Israelites supposed to pay a hired man under the Law of Moses? (Lev. 19:13)

500. How may witnesses were required to testify against an accused sinner according to the Law of Moses? (Deut. 19:15)

501. Who was tested in the "trial" of jealousy, the man or the woman? (Num. 5:14–31)

502. Under the Law of Moses, what could a daughter receive from her father when there was no son? (Num. 27:8)

503. Who found a book of the Law during Josiah's reign? (2 Chron. 34:14)

504. Under the Law of Moses, Israel could eat the beasts that chewed the cud and had what kind of hooves? (Lev. 11:3)

505. If you shed a man's blood, what will you have to shed? (Gen. 9:6)

506. Under the Law of Moses, what was the punishment for both parties taken in adultery? (Lev. 20:10)

507. What was the penalty under the Law of Moses for cursing parents? (Ex. 21:17)

508. How was Israel supposed to judge her neighbors under the requirements of the Law of Moses? (Lev. 19:15)

509. Under the Law of Moses, Israel could eat beasts that had a cloven foot and chewed their what? (Lev. 11:3)

510. What was the penalty for working on the Sabbath under the Law of Moses? (Ex. 31:15)

511. What borrowing law did Nehemiah reform? (Neh. 5:10)

512. Retribution under the Law of Moses required an _____ for an _____. (Ex. 21:24)

513. One who broke the Sabbath under the Law of Moses would be _____ _____ from among his people? (Ex. 31:14)

514. What in the waters could Israel eat under the Law of Moses? (Lev. 11:9)

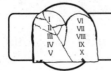
515. The night before manna appeared, what flesh was provided by God? (Ex. 16:13–15)

516. What did the Lord give the Israelites when they complained of constantly eating only manna? (Num. 11:31)

517. Manna was like what seed? (Ex. 16:31)

518. How long did the Lord feed the Israelites manna? (Ex. 16:35)

519. What day of the week did Manna NOT appear for gathering? (Ex. 16:26)

520. What color was Manna? (Ex. 16:31)

521. What did manna taste like? (Ex. 16:31)

522. How long did Israel eat quail rather than manna? (Num. 11:18–20)

523. How many days each week did Manna appear? (Ex. 16:5)

524. How was the Lord's gift of manna to be kept by the Israelites as a remembrance of how He fed them in the wilderness after bringing them out of Egypt? (Ex. 16:32)

525. Israel claimed Moses had brought them out of Egypt to kill them how? (Ex. 16:3)

526. How much manna were the children of Israel to gather on the sixth day of each week? (Ex. 16:5)

527. What did Israel desire rather than manna? (Num. 11:4)

528. What was Manna? (Ex. 16:4, 15)

529. When did manna stop appearing? (Joshua 5:10–12)

530. What happened to manna, if you saved it overnight? (Ex. 16:20)

TRUE OR FALSE

1367. The only weapons that Gideon's army used against the Midianites were their swords. (Judges 7:18)

Solution on page 264

```
T  V  H  V  R  D  K  S  O  L  R
H  R  L  N  A  Q  E  N  X  Q  D
T  R  M  N  V  Y  N  M  N  A  J
S  E  R  P  E  N  T  E  E  Y  Q
V  Z  B  T  N  Q  M  R  V  A  N
E  F  T  W  S  G  B  P  N  I  N
N  M  V  E  D  K  R  N  F  K  L
I  J  T  L  K  U  A  A  G  G  F
S  W  L  V  T  M  N  R  P  G  N
O  X  R  E  R  R  H  G  B  E  R
N  O  T  H  I  N  G  L  P  T  S
```

- David asked Ahimelech to give him something to eat. Ahimelech gave him this hallowed food. (1 Sam. 21:6)

- What food did Moses eat while on Sinai? (Ex. 34:28)

- Adam was told that he would die if he ate the fruit of the tree of knowledge of good and what? (Gen. 2:17)

- What birds fed Elijah by the brook Cherith? (1 Kings 17:4)

- Could Israel eat the "ospray" under the Law of Moses? (Deut. 14:12)

- What did Eve blame for making her eat the forbidden fruit? (Gen. 3:13)

- Under the direction of the Lord,

- Ezekiel baked his barley cakes with this cow's waste. (Ezek. 4:15)

- How many loaves comprised the "shewbread"? (Lev. 24:5)

- Under the Law of Moses, could Israel eat the chamois? (Deut. 14:4–5)

- What sour fruit was used in the proverb about the children's teeth being set on edge? (Ezek. 18:2)

- What did Israel call the Lord's bread? (Ex. 16:15)

- What did Isaac want to eat before he gave his blessing to Esau? (Gen. 27:3)

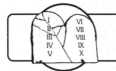

531. Who died because he steadied the Ark of the Covenant of God? (2 Sam. 6:6–7)

532. What was the only thing in the Ark of the Covenant when it was first placed in the temple? (1 Kings 8:9)

533. What priest died at the news of the loss of the Ark of the Covenant? (1 Sam. 4:15, 18)

534. The Ark of the Covenant was placed next to what Philistine god? (1 Sam. 5:2)

535. How many times did the statue of Dagon fall before the Ark of the Covenant? (1 Sam 5:3–4)

536. Who stole the Ark of the Covenant at the death of Eli's sons? (1 Sam. 4:10–11)

537. When Uzzah steadied the Ark of God, what happened? (2 Sam. 6:7)

538. What were the Philistines' golden offerings in the image of when they returned the Ark of the Covenant to Israel? (1 Sam. 6:4)

539. What did God smite the Philistines with for taking the Ark of the Covenant? (1 Sam. 5:2, 6)

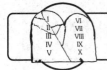
540. What burnt offering did the king of Moab offer on the wall? (2 Kings 3:27)

541. How many sheep were sacrificed by Solomon at the dedication of the temple? (2 Chron. 7:5)

542. What did the Lord "have" for Abel's offering and not Cain's? (Gen. 4:4–5)

543. Whose daughter was offered as a burnt offering to the Lord? (Judges 11:30–39)

544. Jeremiah recorded the Lord's condemnation of the sacrifice of what relations? (Jer. 7:31)

545. What question did Isaac ask Abraham as they prepared to offer sacrifice? (Gen. 22:7)

546. Who was pleased that Abraham would sacrifice his son? (Gen. 22:11–12)

547. Did the Lord have respect for Cain's offering or for Abel's? (Gen. 4:4–5)

548. Who was the first person out of Jephthah's house to greet him, whom he then offered as a sacrifice? (Judges 11:34)

549. Who does Malachi say will yet offer an offering in righteousness? (Mal. 3:3)

550. What was Abel's sacrificial offering to the Lord? (Gen. 4:4)

551. In Jeremiah, God declared that Judah had burned her sons as offerings to what god? (Jer. 19:5)

552. Why did Cain's countenance fall concerning his sacrifice? (Gen. 4:3–5)

553. Isaiah recorded the Lord's opinion of ritualistic offerings by declaring that the Lord was full of what kind of offerings? (Is. 1:11)

554. Which offering of sacrifice under the Law was made as an atonement? (Lev. 1:4)

555. Who will yet offer up a righteous offering unto the Lord? (Mal. 3:3)

556. The Passover lamb is killed on what day of the month Abib? (Ex. 12:6)

557. What was Cain's sacrificial offering to the Lord? (Gen. 4:3)

558. According to Samuel, what is better than sacrifice? (1 Sam. 15:22)

559. The Lord commanded Abraham to use Isaac as what kind of offering? (Gen. 22:2)

560. What offering did God command Abraham to make in Moriah? (Gen. 22:2)

561. What did Elijah pour on his offering during his contest with the priests of Baal? (1 Kings 18:33)

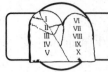
Solution on page 280

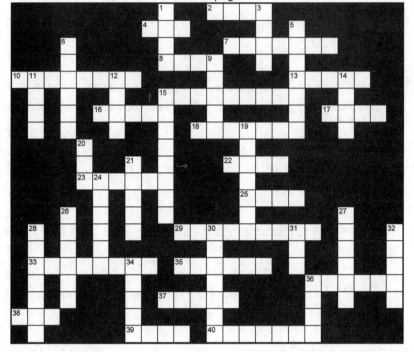

Across

2   When the dove finally returned to the ark as a sign that the waters had receded, it had what part of an olive tree in its beak? (Gen. 8:11)

4   As a sign to Israel, Ezekiel set his face against an iron what? (Ezek. 4:3)

7   When the Lord first appeared to Moses in a bush, what was the bush doing. (Ex. 3:2)

8   Ezekiel lay on which side of his body for 390 days as a sign to Israel. Each day represented a year of Israel's iniquity? (Ezek. 4:4–5)

10   Which king received the sign of a sundial moving backwards to indicate that he would live longer? (Is. 38:4–8)

13   The Lord manifested His acceptance of the tabernacle with a cloud and His _____. (Ex. 40:34)

15   As a sign of his power during Elijah's contest with the priests of Baal, the true God consumed Elijah's what? (1 Kings 18:38)

16   The three faces in common in Ezekiel's two "Cherubim" visions were those of a man, a lion and this bird. (Ezek. 1:10; 10:14)

17   In the vision of Zechariah, a man had

this measuring device in his hand. (Zech. 2:1)

18 As a sign to Israel, Moses put his hand into his bosom. When he withdrew it, what had it become? (Ex. 4:6)

22 In poetic verse, Isaiah stated that in his vision the daughter of _____ would be left as a cottage in a vineyard. (Is. 1:8)

23 The soldiers of what man were chosen to fight the Midianites because they lapped water like a dog. (Judges 7:5–7)

25 Moses saw this burning and it was not consumed. (Ex. 3:2)

29 Did Isaiah have the Lord move the sundial backwards or forwards as a sign to Hezekiah? (2 Kings 20:10)

33 How much of Ezekiel's cut hair did he burn as a sign to Israel? (Ezek. 5:2)

35 To save herself and all in her family from destruction when the Israelites conquered Jericho, Rahab placed a scarlet thread in this aperture. (Joshua 2:18)

36 To determine if God would save Israel by his hand, Gideon devised a test as a sign. On the first morning of this test, he asked God to put dew on a _____, but not on the ground. (Judges 6:37)

37 As a testimony to Israel, the Lord came to Moses in a thick what? (Ex. 19:9)

38 The Lord had Moses turn this into a serpent to use before Pharaoh. (Ex. 4:2–3)

39 In separate visions, John the Revelator was commanded to eat a book and Ezekiel was commanded to eat a what? (Ezek. 3:1)

40 Samuel called unto the Lord, and the Lord sent _____ and rain upon Israel because of its wickedness in desiring a king. (1 Sam. 12:18)

Down

1 To change a serpent back into a rod before Pharaoh, Moses grabbed it by the what? (Ex. 4:4)

3 When the three came out of the fiery furnace, the smell of what element had not "passed" on them? (Dan. 3:26–27)

5 What parts of a man's hand wrote a message to Belshazzar on a wall? (Dan. 5:5)

6 In Ezekiel 10:14 it says, "And every one had four faces: the first face was the face of a _____, and the second . . . a man, . . . the third . . . a lion, and the fourth . . . an eagle."

9 How many years did Isaiah walk "naked and barefoot" as a sign to Egypt and Ethiopia? (Is. 20:3)

11 Obadiah had a vision that concerned what land? (Ob. 1:1)

12 What king refused to ask a sign of the Lord when told to do so by Isaiah? (Is. 7:12)

14 As a sign to the Israelites that they had sinned in asking for a king to rule over them, Samuel called upon the Lord, and the Lord sent thunder and this moisture. (1 Sam. 12:17–18)

15 When Pharaoh's magicians cast down their rods, the rods turned into what? (Ex. 7:12)

19 Noah received this token (it appears

in the heavens). It signified that God would not destroy the earth again by water. (Gen. 9:13–17)

20 Those chosen to fight with Gideon against the Midianites were chosen because they lapped water like this animal. (Judges 7:5)

21 As told by Isaiah, the Lord would give King Ahaz a sign. The sign was the birth of whom? (Is. 7:14)

24 What prophet moved the sundial backwards ten degrees? (2 Kings 20:11)

26 To verify the identity of the woman that would become Isaac's wife, Abraham's servant asked the Lord to have the designated woman water what animals when she was asked? (Gen. 24:14)

27 Who was called by King Belshazzar to interpret the handwriting on the wall? (Dan. 5:13)

28 To stop the murmuring of the Israelites during their journey in the wilderness, what did the Lord make Aaron's rod do? (Num. 17:5)

30 Hezekiah made a pool and this structure to bring water into the city. (2 Kings 20:20)

31 Did the Lord's cloud go before Israel's Exodus camp by day or by night? (Ex. 13:21)

32 What did the army of Gideon lap like a dog as a sign that they were acceptable to the Lord? (Judges 7:5)

34 Ezekiel was by the _____ "Chebar" when he saw his visions. (Ezek. 1:1)

36 How many wings did each of the creatures in Ezekiel's vision have? (Ezek 1:6)

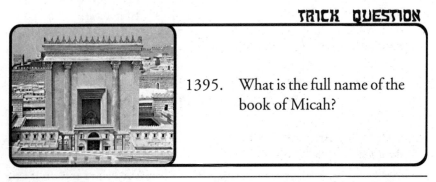

TRICK QUESTION

1395. What is the full name of the book of Micah?

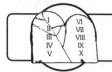
562. What filled the house of the Lord when the Ark was placed in the holy place and the priests withdrew? (1 Kings 8:10)

563. When Cyrus allowed the rebuilding of the temple, he fulfilled the prophecy of what prophet? (Ezra 1:1)

564. What did the king of Tyre receive as yearly payment for his trees that were used in the construction of the temple? (1 Kings 5:9–11)

565. Who did Jeremiah prophesy would authorize the rebuilding of the temple in Jerusalem? (Ezra 1:1–2)

566. At the time of Haggai, the Lord stirred up the _____ of the people to motivate them to build His house. (Haggai 1:14)

567. What was the glory of the Lord described as being like when He accepted the temple of Solomon? (2 Chron. 5:13)

568. Adonijah feared King Solomon and to save himself, he went into the temple and caught hold of the horns of what furnishing? (1 Kings 1:50)

569. Where did Isaiah and Micah prophesy that the Lord's house would be established? (Is. 2:2; Micah 4:1)

570. How many cherubim were in Solomon's temple? (1 Kings 6:23)

---

571. What did the Lord send from heaven to consume the sacrifice at the dedication of Solomon's temple? (2 Chron. 7:1)

572. How many oxen did Solomon offer as a peace offering at the dedication of the temple? (1 Kings 8:63)

573. Who was the first king to build a temple? (1 Kings 6:1)

574. At the dedication of Solomon's temple, the priests could not enter into the edifice because it was filled with what? (2 Chron. 7:2)

575. The "molten sea" in the temple stood upon twelve statues of what animal? (1 Kings 7:25)

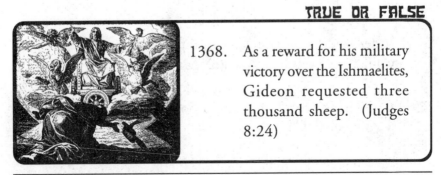

TRUE OR FALSE

1368. As a reward for his military victory over the Ishmaelites, Gideon requested three thousand sheep. (Judges 8:24)

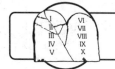
576. What was the color of the "fringes" that the Lord commanded to be attached to the border of the Israelites' garments? (Num. 15:38)

577. The Psalm declares that, "Thou art a priest for ever after the order of _____." (Ps. 110:4)

578. Jethro was a priest in what land? (Ex. 3:1)

579. What is the name of the priest that anointed Solomon king? (1 Kings 1:39)

580. This man and his sons were consecrated to the office of Priest. It was theirs for a "perpetual statute." Who was this man? (Ex. 29:9)

581. What was the retirement age for priesthood workers in the tabernacle? (Num. 8:25)

582. Who succeeded Aaron? (Num. 20:28)

583. What will the sons of Levi yet do according to Malachi? (Mal. 3:3)

584. In what Chapter in 1 Chronicles were the priests divided for work in the temple?

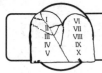

MIRACLES CROSSWORD
Moses, Moses, Moses!

Solution on page 272

Across

3   Elijah would cross Jordan on dry ground by striking it with this piece of his clothing. (2 Kings 2:8)

5   With salt, Elisha healed a spring of what? (2 Kings 2:21)

6   Elijah took the widow's son to this area of her house to raise him from the dead. (1 Kings 17:19)

7   In an attempt to raise a dead child, Elisha gave Gahazi his _____ with instructions to lay it upon the child's face. (2 Kings 4:29)

10 In order to raise a child from the dead, Elisha _____ his body on him. (2 Kings 4:34)

13 To cleanse himself of leprosy, how many times did Naaman dip himself in the river Jordan? (2 Kings 5:14)

14 A little maid told Naaman's wife that in Israel there was a _____ that could heal Naaman of his leprosy. (2 Kings 5:3)

15 Was the widow's child raised from the dead her son or daughter? (1 Kings 17:9, 22)

16 After destroying the prophets of Baal, Elijah told Ahab to eat because there was the "sound of the abundance of" what? (1 Kings 18:41)

18 What direction did the wind come from that the Lord used to part the Red Sea? (Ex. 14:21)

---

114   Challenged by the Old Testament

21 When Elijah struck the river Jordan with his mantle, what did the water do? (2 Kings 2:8)

22 Elijah sent his servant to look toward the sea and the servant saw a little _____ arise that looked like a man's hand. (1 Kings 18:44)

25 Who raised the widow's child from the dead? (1 Kings 17:9, 22)

Down

1 God sent fire from heaven to consume what "offering" during Elijah's contest with the priests of Baal? (1 Kings 18:38)

2 The first miracle Elijah provided for the widow was that the barrel of what food staple would not waste? (1 Kings 17:14)

4 What did God provide for Hagar and Ishmael in the wilderness? (Gen. 21:19)

7 In the first of Moses' miracles before Pharaoh, Aaron's rod _____ the rods of the magicians. (Ex. 7:12)

8 Elisha prayed and asked the Lord to smite the Syrian army with what ailment? (2 Kings 6:18)

9 Elisha told Naaman that to be healed, he should do what seven times in the river Jordan? (2 Kings 5:10)

11 What did the ravens bring to Elijah by the brook Cherith so that he would not hunger? (1 Kings 17:4)

12 When Elisha put meal in a pot of this substance, it healed it so they could eat it. (2 Kings 4:40–41)

16 What is the word used to describe what Israel's king did to his clothes when he read the letter that asked him to heal Naaman? (2 Kings 5:7)

17 During the Exodus, Moses _____ the Red Sea so that Israel could cross on dry ground. (Ex. 14:16)

19 Elisha cast this item into the water to make an axe head swim. (2 Kings 6:6)

20 When Sarah was promised a child in her old age, what did she do? (Gen. 18:12)

23 What did Elisha provide for the widow to pay her debts? (2 Kings 4:1–7)

24 What element did the Lord use to provide quail for the Israelites to eat in the wilderness? (Num. 11:31)

TRICK QUESTION

1396. Other than those acts recorded in 1 Kings, in what book are the acts of Solomon written? (1 Kings 11:41)

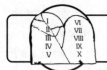
585. What feast is celebrated because of Esther? (Esther 9:27–28)

586. How many days was Israel to eat unleavened bread for the Passover? (Ex. 12:15)

587. The Passover was instituted to memorialize which plague of Egypt? (Ex. 12: 11–12)

588. The feast of Purim was named after what? (Esther 9:26)

589. What celebration did the death of Egypt's firstborn cause to be instituted in Israel? (Ex. 12:11)

590. On which day of the seventh month was the Feast of Tabernacles held? (Lev. 23:34)

591. How many days before the Feast of Tabernacles was the Day of Atonement celebrated? (Lev. 23:27, 34)

592. What did the people dwell in during the Feast of Tabernacles? (Lev. 23:42)

593. What is killed on the fourteenth day of Abib in Israel? (Deut 16:1; Ex. 12:5–6)

594. On what day of the seventh month is the Day of Atonement celebrated? (Lev. 23:27)

595. The Day of Atonement was to be a holy what to the people? (Lev. 23:27)

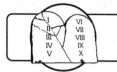

596. None of the people from the Exodus over what age could enter the promised land? (Num. 32:11)

597. What was Caleb's inheritance in the promised land? (Joshua 14:13)

598. How many times did God part the waters before the children of Israel entered the promised land? (Ex. 14:21; Joshua 3:13)

599. Who were the only two of the original Israelites who wandered in the wilderness for forty years that were allowed to enter into the promised land? (Num. 14:38)

600. The Levites received tithes from all Israel in the promised land and did not receive an _____. (Num. 18:24)

601. Why was Moses forbidden to enter the promised land? (Num. 20:8–12)

602. Why did God leave other nations in Canaan after Joshua died? (Judges 2:21–22)

603. What was the name of the spy from the tribe of Judah who was sent to spy out the promised land? (Num. 13:6)

604. What did Joshua and Caleb bring back from the promised land? (Num. 13:23)

605. How long did it take for the "generation of the men of war" to die before Israel could enter the promised land? (Deut. 2:14)

606. Which two tribes requested their inheritance in the promised land NOT over Jordan.? (Num. 32:1, 5)

607. How many portions of the land of promise did the tribe of Joseph receive? (Ezek. 47:13)

608. When did the land enjoy a "Sabbath" under the Law of Moses? (Lev. 25:4)

609. How did the Israelites pass over Jordan after their wanderings in the wilderness? (Joshua 3:17)

610. Which spies from Israel gave a positive report on the promised land? (Num. 14:6–7)

611. What was the name of the spy from the tribe of Ephraim who was chosen to spy out the promised land? (Num. 13:8, 16)

612. What was the method used to divide the "land over Jordan" among the tribes of Israel? (Joshua 14:2)

613. What were the names of the men who were to divide the promised land among the tribes of Israel? (Num. 34:17)

614. Which land was the "promised land" that God gave to Abraham? (Gen. 12:5, 7)

615. What were the Levites given instead of land for their inheritance in the promised land? (Num. 18:24)

616. Which tribes of Israel did Ephraim and Manasseh replace at the division of the promised land? (Joshua 14:4)

617. The promised land given to Abraham was between what two rivers? (Gen. 15:18)

618. What did Joshua and Caleb bring back from the promised land on a stick that they carried between them? (Num. 13:23)

619. How is the land cleansed when it is defiled by the shedding of blood? (Num. 35:33)

620. What did Caleb and Joshua do when Israel refused to enter Canaan? (Num. 14:6)

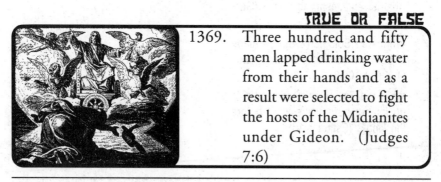

TRUE OR FALSE

1369. Three hundred and fifty men lapped drinking water from their hands and as a result were selected to fight the hosts of the Midianites under Gideon. (Judges 7:6)

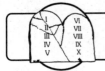

EASY TRIVIA MATCH GAME

Moses, Moses, Moses!

Match the questions on the left with the answers on the right. The solution is on page 262

A. Isaiah advises us to seek the Lord while he may be _____. (Is. 55:6)

B. Which of Jacob's sons did Potiphar the Egyptian purchase? (Gen. 37:36)

C. Jeremiah declared that the earth was without form and _____. (Jer. 4:23)

D. The Preacher declared that to everything there is a _____ and a time. (Eccl. 3:1)

E. Who is the author of Proverbs? (Prov. 1:1)

F. What did the men of Anathoth seek from Jeremiah? (Jer. 11:21)

G. What is the first word in the *Old Testament*? (Gen. 1:1)

H. What was Elisha doing when Elijah first found him? (1 Kings 19:19)

I. What did Adam and Eve make for themselves to cover their nakedness? (Gen. 3:7)

J. According to Genesis, what is Adams relationship to Eve? (Gen. 3:6)

K. What was Solomon's throne made of before it was covered with gold? (1 Kings 10:18)

L. What did Esther ask her people to do for her before she went before the king? (Esther 4:16)

Ivory

In

Joseph

Aprons

Solomon

Season

Husband

Found

His life

Plowing

Fast

Void

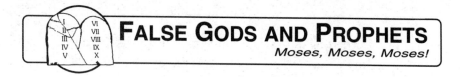
621. One of the condemnations by God against Judah was that they worshiped "the works of their own" what? (Jer. 1:16)

622. Speaking of false prophets, the Lord said he would "feed them with wormwood, and make them drink the water of" what? (Jer. 23:15)

623. The Lord declared that there were wicked men among his people who set traps and snares to catch whom? (Jer. 5:26)

624. The Lord declared to sinful Judah, that they trusted in what kind of deceitful words, that could not profit? (Jer. 7:8)

625. In her apostasy, Judah made "cakes to the queen" of what place? (Jer. 7:18)

626. The statue of Dagon did this before the Ark of God. (1 Sam. 5:3)

627. Did Balaam bless or curse Israel? (Num. 23:11)

628. The false prophet Hananiah broke Jeremiah's yoke of wood, so the Lord said he would put yokes of what metal on the Israelites instead? (Jer. 28:13)

629. Isaiah declared that the prophet who teaches lies is not the head, but the what? (Is. 9:15)

630. Dagon was the name of the god of what people? (1 Sam. 5:2)

---

631. The Lord is against those who "prophesy false dreams... and cause my people to err" by the prophets what? (Jer. 23:32)

632. Micah declared that the evil prophets divined for what? (Micah 3:11)

633. What were the wise men of Chaldea unable to do for Nebuchadnezzar? (Dan. 2:6, 10)

634. What did God's fire consume during Elijah's contest with the wicked priests of Baal? (1 Kings 18:38)

635. What did Jeroboam sacrifice to in Bethel, that had replaced sacrifice to the God of Israel in Jerusalem? (1 Kings 12:32)

636. Who did Balak ask to go and curse Israel? (Num. 22:5–6)

637. The Lord told the people of Judah that their false gods were as plentiful as their what? (Jer. 2:28)

638. Chemosh was the false god of what country? (1 Kings 11:7)

639. What did the Israelites have Aaron make while Moses was on Sinai? (Ex. 32:3–4)

640. What metal did Aaron use to make an idol for his people? (Ex. 32:3–4)

641. The Lord declared to Zephaniah that he would cut off those that worshiped the host of _____. (Zeph. 1:5)

642. The children of Israel, at the time of Hezekiah, burned incense to the "brasen serpent" Moses had made. What did they name the image? (2 Kings 18:4)

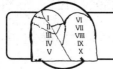

643. What is the ninth commandment? (Ex. 20:16)

644. Why were the Israelites commanded that they could not vex any strangers among them? (Ex. 22:21)

645. What is the sixth commandment? (Ex. 20:13)

646. How many commandments were given by the Lord from Sinai? (Ex. 20:3–17)

647. What is the fifth of the ten commandments? (Ex. 20:12)

648. What is the seventh commandment? (Ex. 20:14)

649. What were Lot and his family commanded NOT to do as they fled from Sodom? (Gen. 19:17)

650. God said that man was to cleave unto his what? (Gen. 2:24)

651. What is the tenth and last of the ten commandments? (Ex. 20:17)

652. What is the fourth commandment? (Ex. 20:8)

653. What was the first commandment given from Sinai? (Ex. 20:3)

654. As the book of Numbers opens, the Lord commands Moses to take the _____ of all the congregation. (Num. 1:2)

655. How often did God command the people of Israel to meditate upon the book of the Law? (Joshua 1:8)

656. After _____ died, the Lord commanded Joshua to cross over Jordan. (Joshua 1:2)

657. Who commanded Elijah to go to the brook Cherith? (1 Kings 17:2–3)

658. What is the third commandment? (Ex. 20:7)

659. What is the second commandment? (Ex. 20:4)

660. What is the eighth commandment? (Ex. 20:15)

661. Who commanded Noah to build an Ark? (Gen. 6:13–14)

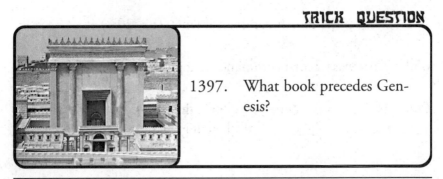

TRICK QUESTION

1397. What book precedes Genesis?

The Land
They Lived In

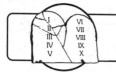

VI

662. What was the name of the mount in Deuteronomy from which Moses viewed the promised land? (Deut. 32:49)

663. Which plain did Lot choose when he and Abraham went their separate ways? (Gen. 13:11)

664. What land did Cain live in after God cursed him and he went out from His presence? (Gen. 4:16)

665. Isaiah said the land of Judah would be a terror to what nation? (Is. 19:17)

666. What was the former name of Bethel? (Gen. 28:19)

667. Into what country was Joseph sold into slavery? (Gen. 37:36)

668. The vision of Obadiah concerns the people and land of what nation? (Ob. 1:1)

669. Where did Moses go after he killed an Egyptian and fled from Egypt? (Ex. 2:15)

670. What was the wilderness called between Elim and Sinai? (Ex. 16:1)

671. What was the first city conquered by Israel after crossing the river Jordan? (Joshua 3:16; 6:2, 20)

672. Cyrus was king of what country? (Dan. 10:1)

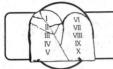

CITY LOCATION MAP
The Land They Lived In

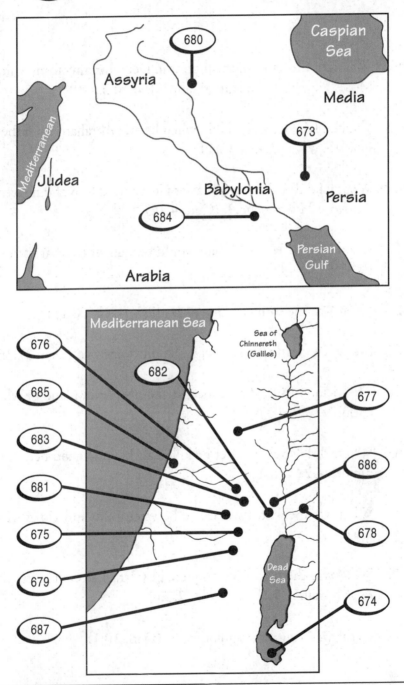

673. What was the name of the palace city of Artaxerxes? (Neh. 1:1)

674. Abraham bartered with the Lord in an attempt to save which two cities? (Gen. 18:20–24)

675. Which is the City of David? (2 Sam. 5:6–7)

676. Jacob changed the name of Luz to what? (Gen. 28:19)

677. Joseph's bones were carried from Egypt with the Exodus and buried in what city? (Joshua 24:32)

678. To what city did Lot flee in order to avoid dying in the destruction of Sodom? (Gen. 19:22)

679. When Naomi and Ruth went to Israel to live, in what city did they make their home? (Ruth 1:22)

680. Nahum prophesied of the burden of what city? (Nahum 1:1)

681. What is the name of the only city that made peace with Israel (before the land was divided among the tribes)? (Joshua 11:19)

682. Rahab the harlot lived in what city? (Joshua 2:1)

683. What was Jeremiah's home town? (Jer. 1:1)

684. Where was Abraham born? (Gen. 11:27–28)

685. From what city-port did Jonah depart to go to Tarshish? (Jonah 1:3)

686. What was the second city conquered by the Israelites after they crossed the river Jordan? (Joshua 8:1–2, 28)

687. The city name of Kirjatharba was changed to what? (Judges 1:10)

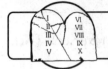
688. What did Ezra receive from Artaxerxes which gave him the authority to return to Jerusalem? (Ezra 7:11)

689. When Nehemiah heard of the plight of his brethren in Jerusalem, he mourned and _____. (Neh. 1:4)

690. What did Nehemiah want to build at Jerusalem? (Neh. 2:17)

691. Ezekiel said those living in Jerusalem during its siege would die by what method? (Ezek. 6:12)

692. How many times did Nehemiah visit Jerusalem? (Neh. 2:5; 13:6–7)

693. How did David lead the Ark of God into Jerusalem? (2 Sam. 6:16)

694. In poetic verse, Isaiah prophesied that in the last days, what is to go out from Jerusalem? (Is. 2:3)

695. To stop the destruction of Jerusalem, Jeremiah told Zedekiah that he had to do what? (Jer. 38:17)

696. Who did Zechariah declare would enter Jerusalem riding on a colt? (Zech. 9:9)

697. Children from what four tribes of Israel dwelt in Jerusalem? (1 Chron. 9:3)

698. Who was the governor in Jerusalem at the time of Haggai? (Haggai 1:1)

699. What did Cyrus authorize the rebuilding of in Jerusalem? (Ezra 1:2)

700. What day did Nehemiah close Jerusalem's gates to merchants? (Neh. 13:19)

TRUE OR FALSE

1370. Ahab had Jehoshaphat disguise himself in battle to avoid being killed. (1 Kings 22:30)

Solution on page 257

```
J  Y  R  M  G  N  V  R  L  F  U  Z
E  L  C  T  G  X  M  H  E  Z  D  T
R  B  X  L  F  I  S  R  V  T  R  W
I  N  R  Z  G  E  L  Y  I  H  T  A
C  F  R  Z  D  O  T  G  S  N  P  C
H  T  V  A  D  N  M  I  A  P  K  A
O  R  K  M  E  M  H  O  O  L  F  B
L  D  R  W  C  S  I  J  R  L  D  U
N  K  T  X  R  B  T  Z  N  R  T  L
X  H  C  A  Y  N  M  J  P  W  A  G
B  E  T  H  L  E  H  E  M  A  B  H
P  T  X  M  M  S  O  D  O  M  H  L
```

- How many cities did Solomon give Hiram for providing supplies for the temple? (1 Kings 9:11)

- What was the home town of David? (1 Sam. 16:1, 4)

- Saul was made king of Israel in what city? (1 Sam. 11:15)

- What did Hiram call the twenty cities given to him by Solomon? (1 Kings 9:13)

- Where did Miriam die? (Num. 20:1)

- What land did Job come from? (Job 1:1)

- Where did Jeremiah go when he was set free by Babylon? (Jer. 40:6)

- What city's wall fell down to allow Israel to conquer the city? (Joshua 6:2, 20)

- Where did Jonah flee, rather than go to Nineveh? (Jonah 1:3)

- The two famous cities that were near the Plain of Jordan where Lot lived were _____ and _____. (Gen. 13:10)

- Which tribe received forty-eight cities in the promised land as an inheritance? (Joshua 21:41)

- In what city did Jonah board a ship so that he could flee from the Lord? (Jonah 1:3)

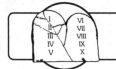

701. In Numbers, what was the name of the Mount from which Moses saw the promised land? (Num. 27:12)

702. What was the name of the mount where Elijah's contest between the gods was held? (1 Kings 18:19)

703. Moses saw the promised land from Mt. Abarim in the book of Numbers, and from Mt. Nebo and Mt. _____ in Deuteronomy. (Deut. 3:27)

704. For what event are the mountains of Ararat known? (Gen. 8:4)

705. What did seventy of the elders of Israel see when they were with Moses on Sinai? (Ex. 24:9–10)

706. How long did Moses stay on the mount the first time? (Ex. 24:18)

707. Noah's ark came to rest where? (Gen. 8:4)

708. What did the people hear and see on Mount Sinai before Moses spoke with God? (Ex. 19:16)

709. Did Ezekiel bless or curse Mount Seir? (Ezek. 35)

710. What is the name of the mountain where Aaron died? (Num. 20:27–28)

711. Zechariah prophesied that this mount would cleave in two at the Second Coming. (Zech. 14:4)

712. What was on Sinai when the Lord descended upon it in fire? (Ex. 19:18)

713. Micah declared that the Lord would eventually reign from what mount? (Micah 4:7)

714. Isaiah, speaking in poetic form, states that the mountain will do what at the coming of the Lord? (Isa. 64:1)

715. What was the total time Moses spent on the mount when he received the Law from the Lord? (Ex. 24:18; 34:28)

716. According to Isaiah, where is the mountain of the Lord's house to be established? (Is. 2:2)

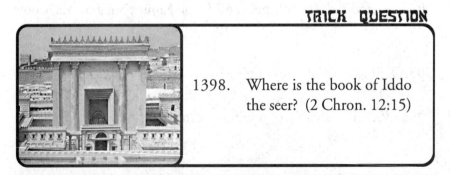

TRICK QUESTION

1398. Where is the book of Iddo the seer? (2 Chron. 12:15)

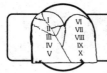

MATCHING CITIES
The Land They Lived In

Match the questions on the left with the answers on the right. The solution is on page 269.

A. What is the name of the future holy city that Ezekiel described? (Ezek. 48:35)

B. When Abraham bartered with the Lord to save Sodom from destruction, what was the lowest number of righteous men he used? (Gen. 18:32)

C. Did Hiram like the twenty cities King Solomon gave him? (1 Kings 9:12)

D. How many cities of refuge were there in Israel after the division of land among the tribes of Israel? (Joshua 20:7–8)

E. Nineveh's population was more than this number? (Jonah 4:11)

F. How many times did the Israelites march around Jericho on the seventh day? (Joshua 6:4)

G. Where was Rahab's house located in Jericho? (Joshua 2:15)

H. What occurred at the battle of Jericho at the blast of the ram's horn? (Joshua 6:5)

I. Who lived in Sodom and Gomorrah that Abraham wanted to save from destruction? (Gen. 19:1)

J. When Abraham bartered with the Lord to save Sodom from destruction, what number of righteous men did he start with? (Gen. 18:24)

K. What did the Lord name the locale where a tower was being built to reach heaven? (Gen. 11:4, 9)

Lot

Babel

The LORD is there

No

The people shouted

Fifty

Ten

120,000

Six

On the city wall

Seven

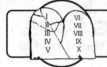
*Match the questions on the left with the answers on the
right. The solution is on page 273.*

A. Noah's Ark was made of what wood?
(Gen. 6:14)

Nimrod

B. Who did Absalom kill because he
had defiled his sister? (2 Sam.
13:28–29)

Scrip

C. In poetic prophecy, Isaiah declared
that the people of this tribe would
be a terror to Egypt. (Is. 19:17)

Cupbearer

D. In what capacity was Nehemiah em-
ployed by Artaxerxes? (Neh. 1:11)

Herdsman

E. What was Amos' occupation? (Amos
1:1)

Naaman

F. Who was captain of the hosts of
Syria at the time of Elisha? (2 Kings
5:1)

Judah

G. Amos was a herdsman in what land?
(Amos 1:1)

Ammon

H. Who is known as the "mighty hunter"
of Genesis? (Gen. 10:9)

Tekoa

I. David put five stones in his
shepherd's bag to fight Goliath. What
did he call the bag? (1 Sam. 17:40)

Gopher Wood

Kings, Rulers,
And Such

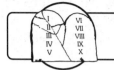

VII

717. What name did Zephaniah call the black robed priests of Baal in the kingdom of Judah? (Zeph. 1:4)

718. What kingdom was represented by the stone in Nebuchadnezzar's dream? (Dan. 2:44–45)

719. Which kingdom conquered Israel and carried off its people, thereby putting an end to Israel as a kingdom? (2 Kings 18:9–10)

720. Which kingdom did Assyria carry into captivity in 721 BC? (2 Kings 17:6)

721. Was Israel divided into two kingdoms at the prophet Hosea's time? (Hosea 1:1)

722. What was the name of the king of Babylon who captured Judah during Jeremiah's time? (Jer. 21:7)

723. What was the name of the Ephraimite that was promised ten pieces of the kingdom of Israel? (1 Kings 11:31)

724. How many provinces comprised the kingdom of Ahasuerus at the time of Esther? (Esther 1:1)

725. In Nebuchadnezzar's dream, what kingdom was represented by the head of the man-image? (Dan. 2:37–38)

726. The armies of what country carried the Kingdom of Israel into captivity? (2 Kings 17:6)

727. Which kingdom of Israel did Amos prophesy would be carried into captivity? (Amos 7:11)

728. Darius was king of what empire? (Dan. 5:31)

729. The "burden of Egypt" is in what chapter in Isaiah?

730. How did Isaiah dress for three years as a "sign and wonder" to Egypt and Ethiopia? (Is. 20:3)

731. Why did Samuel take away Saul's kingdom? (1 Sam. 13:9, 13–14)

732. What nations did the two sisters, Aholoh and Aholibah, represent? (Ezek. 23:4)

733. Jacob and his family were assigned to dwell in what part of Egypt? (Gen. 45:10)

734. Which kingdom of Israel did Hosea prophesy would survive? Hosea 1:7)

TRUE OR FALSE

1371. To raise the widow's dead son, Elijah stretched himself two times upon him. (1 Kings 17:21)

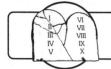
804. Haman desired to destroy all the what? (Esther 3:8–10)

805. Korah and his followers rebelled against Moses, so the Lord destroyed them when the earth opened up and did what? (Num. 16:31–32)

806. The plague of locusts that the Lord commanded Moses to bring upon Egypt ate all that had not been destroyed by the what? (Ex. 10:12)

807. God declared to the people of Judah that like destroying lions, their own swords had devoured their what? (Jer. 2:30)

808. The Lord destroyed the Egyptians who followed the Israelites during the Exodus by drowning them in the what? (Ex. 14:28)

809. Hosea said the reason God's people would be destroyed was because of their lack of what? (Hosea 4:6)

810. God destroyed Sodom and Gomorrah by raining what from heaven? (Gen. 19:24)

811. David declared that he would destroy Goliath to prove there was a _____ in Israel. (1 Sam. 17:46)

812. Hosea prophesied that the kingdom of what people would be destroyed. (Hosea 1:4)

813. The sons of what tribe gathered near to Moses at the base of Sinai after Moses destroyed the golden calf? (Ex. 32:26)

KINGS WORD SEARCH

Kings, Rulers, And Such

Solution on page 268

```
J  F  D  N  J  E  R  O  B  O  A  M  F  M  W
W  D  A  R  I  U  S  A  H  A  B  G  K  R  D
L  W  H  J  M  A  N  A  S  S  E  H  A  R  A
K  M  P  E  L  O  Y  K  K  Q  F  Z  A  G  V
M  A  M  H  M  C  Y  R  U  S  Z  Z  H  M  I
Q  L  B  O  P  K  R  C  Y  E  Z  T  H  S  D
L  B  L  I  R  H  Z  E  N  A  E  K  E  Q  J
X  O  F  A  M  L  T  D  H  H  R  X  Z  F  T
S  D  D  K  L  E  A  S  S  O  R  G  E  R  N
R  T  C  I  P  H  L  O  J  E  B  W  K  G  K
X  S  M  M  C  E  B  E  X  W  L  O  I  B  R
R  J  A  U  B  H  K  A  C  N  K  Z  A  H  H
Y  W  B  U  S  Y  T  W  V  H  M  L  H  M  M
D  E  W  I  L  R  W  A  D  O  N  I  J  A  H
N  V  R  B  A  L  V  R  N  N  K  T  K  F  W
```

- Who was king in Persia during the time of Nehemiah? (Neh. 2:1)

- Which King of Persia authorized the rebuilding of the temple at Jerusalem? (Ezra 1:2)

- Who was the first king of Israel? (1 Sam. 9:17)

- Who did Samuel anoint to be king in Saul's place? (1 Sam. 16:1, 13)

- What king did Daniel prophesy would eat grass like an ox? (Dan. 4:32–33)

- Who was the king of the Kingdom of Israel at the time of Hosea? (Hosea 1:1)

- Which of Gideon's sons was made king over Israel? (Judges 9:1–3)

- To heal his sickness, what king petitioned the Lord saying he had walked in truth, with a perfect heart, and done that which was good? (2 Kings 20:3)

- Who was the third king of Israel? (1 Kings 1:39)

- Elijah is introduced in the scriptures when he prophesies to what wicked king? (1 Kings 17:1)

- What was the name of the first king over the kingdom of Judah after the division of Israel? (1 Kings 12:21)

- Who was king in Jerusalem when Nebuchadnezzar came to besiege it? (Dan. 1:1)

- What king saw the writing on the wall? (Dan. 5:1, 5)

- Who was the king in Persia that followed Cyrus? (Ezra 4:5)

- What is the name of Saul's son who was made a king? (2 Sam. 2:10)

- Which of David's sons made himself king when David was old? (1 Kings 1:5)

- Which of Hezekiah's sons reigned for fifty-five years? (2 Kings 21:1)

- Which king of the Amalekites did Saul save, contrary to God's command? (1 Sam. 15:8)

TRICK QUESTION

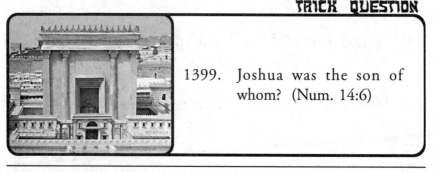

1399. Joshua was the son of whom? (Num. 14:6)

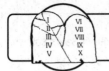
735. Isaiah prophesied that the government would eventually be upon whose shoulders? (Is. 9:6)

736. Which two and one-half tribes took their inheritance on the east side of Jordan? (Num. 34:14–15)

737. How many tribes did Jeroboam rule over? (1 Kings 11:31)

738. The people of Israel requested Samuel to give them a what, like other nations? (1 Sam. 8:5)

739. When the kingdom of Israel split in two, the southern portion was called the kingdom of what? (1 Kings 12:23–24)

740. What were the names of the first two kings of divided Israel? (1 Kings 11:31, 43)

741. What did Jethro suggest to help Moses in governing Israel? (Ex. 18:24–25)

742. Saul was a descendant from which tribe of Israel? (1 Sam. 9:1–2)

743. Gideon descended from which tribe of Israel? (Judges 6:13–15)

744. Which two tribes of Israel followed King Rehoboam? (1 Kings 12:21)

745. What prophet prophesied to Jeroboam that Israel would be divided into two kingdoms? (1 Kings 11:30–31)

746. Hosea prophesied the end of which kingdom of Israel? (Hosea 1:4)

747. What were the rulers of Israel called after the judges? (1 Sam. 8:20)

748. What did the Lord "raise up" to rule Israel after Joshua died? (Judges 2:16)

TRUE OR FALSE

1372. After being warned of their imminent destruction, the people of Nineveh proclaimed a fast, because they believed in God. (Jonah 3:5)

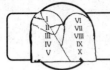
749. The author of Ecclesiastes claims to be the son of what king? (Eccl. 1:1)

750. Nebuchadnezzar was king of what country? (Dan. 1:1)

751. Which king had seven hundred wives and three hundred concubines? (1 Kings 11:1, 3)

752. Who was the king in Israel before Ahab? (1 Kings 16:28)

753. At the time of Nehemiah, what king's royal city was named Shushan? (Neh. 1:1; 2:1)

754. Who was the king in Persia at the time of Ezra? (Ezra 7:1)

755. What was the name of the first king over the ten tribes (or the kingdom of Israel)? (1 Kings 11:30–31)

756. Which king requested that a servant kill him so he could avoid being killed by a woman? (Judges 9:53–54)

757. Jezebel was the wife of which king in Israel? (1 Kings 16:29, 31)

758. Who was anointed king over all Israel after David? (1 Kings 1:39)

759. Which king in Judah was so righteous that it was said his heart was perfect with the Lord all his days? (1 Kings 15:14)

760. Which king in Israel reigned only seven days and then killed himself by burning the king's house around him? (1 Kings 16:15–18)

761. Which king of Israel broke Moses' "brasen serpent" into pieces? (2 Kings 18:1, 4)

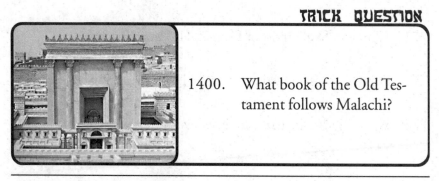

TRICK QUESTION

1400. What book of the Old Testament follows Malachi?

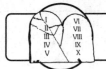

762. How long did Eli judge Israel? (1 Sam. 4:18)

763. What did Isaiah first tell Hezekiah concerning his illness? (2 Kings 20:1)

764. Psalm 23: What did the Lord "restoreth" to David? (Ps. 23:3)

765. Who was killed before King Zedekiah's eyes? (2 Kings 25:7)

766. Who was the first Nazarite judge in Israel? (Judges 13:5, 24)

767. How long did Zedekiah reign in Jerusalem? (Jer. 52:1)

768. What did the people shout when Samuel presented them with their first king? (1 Sam. 10:24)

769. How long did David reign over the tribe of Judah before becoming king over all Israel? (2 Sam. 2:11)

770. What was the name of the Babylonian king who captured the kingdom of Judah? (2 Kings 24:1)

771. Why was Saul afraid of David? (1 Sam. 18:12)

772. How old was Zedekiah when he became king? (Jer. 52:1)

773. Which judge in Israel had his eyes put out? (Judges 16:20–21)

774. What was the fate of the Amalekite who claimed he killed King Saul? (2 Sam. 1:15)

775. What king reigned over the Israelites who dwelled in the cities of Judah after the division of Israel into two kingdoms? (1 Kings 12:17)

776. What happened to the Canaanite kings when they heard about the river Jordan stopping? (Joshua 5:1)

777. Who was Israel's second king? (1 Sam. 16:1, 13)

778. How many years did Saul reign before God took his kingdom? (1 Sam. 13:1, 14)

779. Who was the first king of Israel that wanted to build a house for God to dwell in? (2 Sam. 7:1–5)

780. What king was to grow hair like eagle's feathers? (Dan. 4:33)

781. Who rejected Saul from being the king over Israel? (1 Sam. 15:23)

TRUE OR FALSE

1373. The name of Moses' father-in-law is Reuel. (Ex. 2:16–21)

Solution on page 277

```
E  P  R  T  E  L  I  J  A  H  W  Y  F  Y  B
N  R  B  V  J  R  N  T  K  W  C  G  G  N  E
J  E  R  D  V  U  R  T  X  Q  N  A  O  P  Z
O  M  B  D  A  H  D  D  P  X  R  S  H  R  R
S  C  M  U  T  R  O  A  L  N  M  L  D  A  A
H  T  T  J  C  O  I  E  H  A  Z  I  G  J  B
U  M  W  W  G  H  B  U  S  L  V  L  P  H  E
A  J  O  M  V  E  A  L  S  A  L  E  M  E  J
C  M  F  T  Z  F  Y  D  D  K  Q  R  R  Z  S
B  Q  U  E  S  T  I  O  N  S  F  H  M  E  O
N  M  J  D  P  B  T  H  W  E  T  L  H  K  L
B  E  L  S  H  A  Z  Z  A  R  Z  N  Y  I  O
R  E  H  O  B  O  A  M  A  M  L  Z  R  A  M
O  T  H  N  I  E  L  E  T  M  X  J  A  H  O
M  M  L  M  F  C  H  Q  V  P  R  R  N  R  N
```

- Who did Ahab tell about what had occurred after Elijah's contest with the wicked priests of Baal? (1 Kings 19:1)

- Under the rule of the judges, who was the first judge in Israel? (Judges 3:9)

- Who appointed Zedekiah king in Judah? (2 Kings 24:10, 17)

- How many tribes of Israel did Rehoboam rule over? (1 Kings 12:21)

- Which judge of Israel killed more enemies at his death than during his life? (Judges 16:29–30)

- Which prophet did King Ahab accuse of troubling Israel? (1 Kings 18:17)

- Which of Jacob's sons received the kingship blessing? (Gen. 49:10)

- To whom did Artaxerxes give a letter allowing the people of Israel (including the priests and Levites) to return to Jerusalem? (Ezra 7:11)

- Rehoboam would not reduce the tax upon the Israelites, so they rebelled against the house of whom? (1 Kings 12:19)

- Over what country was Melchizedek king? (Gen. 14:18)

- Who was king after Nebuchadnezzar? (Dan. 5:1–2)

- What king conquered Belshazzar? (Dan. 5:31)

- Which king asked God for a longer life? (Is. 38:5)

- Was Hezekiah a good or an evil king? (2 Kings 18:3)

- What was the name of Solomon's son who reigned after him? (1 Kings 11:43)

- The Queen of Sheba went to visit Solomon to prove him with hard what? (1 Kings 10:1)

- Of which king was it said that he did more to provoke the Lord than all the kings that were before him? (1 Kings 16:33)

- Who followed Moses as Israel's leader? (Num. 27:18)

- How many kings of Judah ruled during the time of the prophet Micah? (Micah 1:1)

- Isaiah declared that Israel's leaders would cause the people to do what? (Is. 9:16)

- Who sought to kill Jeroboam to prevent him from being King of the ten tribes? (1 Kings 11:40)

- After Solomon became king, he prayed that God would give him an understanding what? (1 Kings 3:9)

TRICK QUESTION

1401. When the people of Israel asked for a king, who did the Lord say they had rejected? (1 Sam. 8:7)

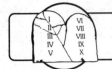
782. Who did Deborah choose to lead Israel's army? (Judges 4:6)

783. What did the Philistines do after the death of Goliath? (1 Sam. 17:51)

784. Who finally agreed to fight Goliath? (1 Sam. 17:31–32)

785. Where did David instruct Joab to place Uriah in the battle? (2 Sam. 11:15)

786. Who slew Jonathan? (1 Sam. 31:2)

787. As the Assyrian army besieged Judah, the Lord promised that a what, would escape out of Jerusalem? (2 Kings 19:31)

788. What was the request of Balak to Balaam concerning Israel? (Num. 22:4, 6)

789. Who smote the camp of the Assyrians in Isaiah and killed one hundred and eighty-five thousand warriors? (Is. 37:36)

790. How were Moses' hands kept in the air so Israel could win its battle over Amalek? (Ex. 17:12)

791. What woman did Barak ask to go to war with him? (Judges 4:4, 8)

792. What leadership position did Gideon turn down after his victory over the Midianites? (Judges 8:22–23)

793. Benaiah, one of David's great warriors, slew an Egyptian of great stature with the Egyptian's own what? (1 Chron. 11:23)

794. What did David gather from a brook before he went to fight Goliath? (1 Sam. 17:40)

795. Who led Israel into the battle against Amalek during the Exodus? (Ex. 17:9)

796. What giant challenged Israel to a single-man combat? (1 Sam. 17:4)

797. What did the Lord cause the Syrian army to hear that frightened them so much that they fled? (2 Kings 7:6)

798. According to Zechariah, what number of nations will be gathered against Jerusalem in the day of the Lord? (Zech. 14:2)

799. What was the rash vow Jephthah made in order to defeat the Ammonites? (Judges 11:31)

800. When the Israelites fought Amalek during their wanderings, what determined the victory? (Ex. 17:11)

801. Who smote the army of the Assyrians under Sennacherib? (2 Kings 19:35)

802. Who delivered Israel from the Midianites? (Judges 7:14)

803. What General used trumpets against the army of the Midianites? (Judges 7:18)

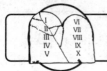

814. What did Jacob put on in order to deceive his father, so that his skin would feel like Esau's skin? (Gen. 27:16)

815. What did God say he would slay if Pharaoh refused to let Israel go? (Ex. 4:23)

816. In Isaiah, what army did it say "arose" in the morning "dead corpses"? (Is. 37:36)

817. Who did the king of Babylon kill before Zedekiah's eyes? (Jer. 39:6)

818. According to 2 Samuel, what was the nationality of the man who killed Saul? (2 Sam. 1:5–10)

819. Whose two sons were killed for offering "strange" fire? (Lev. 10:1–2)

820. What did the Philistines do to Saul's body? (1 Sam. 31:10)

821. Who did Jacob pretend to be so that he would gain the birthright blessing? (Gen. 27:19)

822. Who built a golden image and commanded that when a trumpet sounded, all should worship it? (Dan. 3:5)

823. Under the Law of Moses, the penalty for cursing whom was death? (Ex. 21:17)

824. Who gained the birthright blessing from Isaac through subtlety? (Gen. 27:35–36)

825. Who killed the giant that had six fingers and six toes? (2 Sam. 21:20–21)

826. How old was Joshua when he died? (Joshua 24:29)

827. How old was Methuselah when he died? (Gen. 5:27)

828. Who did Elisha raise from the dead? (2 Kings 4:8, 35)

829. Who conjured up Samuel from the dead for Saul? (1 Sam. 28:7, 11)

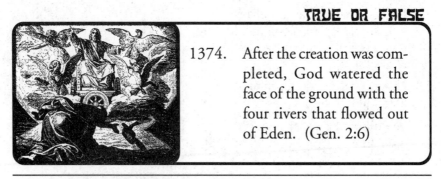

TRUE OR FALSE

1374. After the creation was completed, God watered the face of the ground with the four rivers that flowed out of Eden. (Gen. 2:6)

Solution on page 261

```
N  I  N  E  T  Y  E  I  G  H  T  E
J  K  G  N  B  E  H  E  A  D  E  D
A  M  M  R  N  J  G  R  P  R  S  N
C  J  H  I  E  N  E  N  T  H  H  A
O  X  M  F  I  U  O  W  T  E  D  B
B  A  S  K  I  I  B  I  S  Z  A  O
F  T  O  S  L  R  W  E  L  E  R  T
D  P  L  L  W  N  E  K  N  K  T  H
Y  M  O  L  N  O  C  B  K  I  S  C
M  C  M  Q  N  E  R  B  A  A  L  B
W  G  O  D  N  T  R  D  R  H  K  G
L  M  N  K  M  O  R  D  E  C  A  I
```

- Before he was killed, Absalom hung helpless by his head in the branch of what large plant? (2 Sam. 18:9)

- Haman prepared a gallows for whom? (Esther 7:10)

- What people did Haman want to destroy? (Esther 3:8–10)

- Gehazi placed the staff of Elisha on a dead child as instructed. Did it raise the dead child from the dead? (2 Kings 4:31)

- Eli died when he fell and broke his what? (I Sam. 4:18)

- How old was Eli when he died? (1 Sam. 4:15)

- The Lord slew Nadab and Abihu, the sons of Aaron, because they offered what strange element to the Lord? (Lev. 10:1–2)

- Who ordered Joab's death? (1 Kings 2:29–31)

- Isaiah told which king of Israel that he was going to die? (Is. 38:1)

- Jeremiah prophesied that the false prophets would die by the sword and by what natural disaster? (Jer. 14:15)

- What person did Job declare he would yet see, even after worms destroyed his body? (Job. 19:26)

- Which of Jacob's sons told Jacob he could slay his own two sons if he did not bring Benjamin back from Egypt? (Gen. 42:37)

- It is recorded that with his bare hands, Samson killed a what? (Judges 14:5–6)

- Ishbosheth, Saul's son, died when he was _____. (2 Sam. 4:7)

- Amos prophesied that Israel would be led away captive, and Jeroboam would die by this weapon. (Amos 7:11)

- As Absalom hung in the tree, Joab thrust him in the heart with three of these weapons. (2 Sam. 18:14)

- Who did Jezebel have stoned to death so that she could give his vineyard to Ahab? (1 Kings 21:6, 13)

- Absalom contrived a conspiracy against David so that he could become what? (2 Sam. 15:10)

- The first lie by Samson to Delilah concerning the source of his strength was to bind him with seven green what? (Judges 16:7)

- Who covered himself with the skins of kids so as to feel like his hairy brother and deceive his father? (Gen. 27:16–23)

- Speaking through Jeremiah, the Lord said Israel's prophets spoke by what false prophet? (Jer. 2:8)

TRICK QUESTION

1402. After the death of Solomon, the people came to Rehoboam and requested that he make the heavy "yoke" placed upon them by Solomon _____. (1 Kings 12:4)

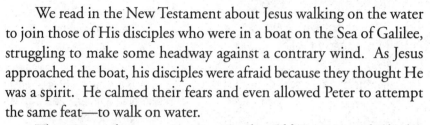

We read in the New Testament about Jesus walking on the water to join those of His disciples who were in a boat on the Sea of Galilee, struggling to make some headway against a contrary wind. As Jesus approached the boat, his disciples were afraid because they thought He was a spirit. He calmed their fears and even allowed Peter to attempt the same feat—to walk on water.

There is another amazing story in the *Old Testament* which also describes a suspension of the law of gravity. As the story goes, the "sons of the prophets" wanted some additional living space, so they asked Elisha if it was all right for them to go to the river Jordan and clear a space for a new dwelling. Elisha agreed with their plan, simply stating, "Go ye." However, the men wanted Elisha to go with them and support them in their project, and he answered, "I will go."

The group went to the banks of the river Jordan and began felling trees with Elisha in their midst. As one of the workers cut down a beam, the head of his axe sailed from the axe handle and went into the river. The worker immediately became distraught and cried out to Elisha, "Alas, master! For it was borrowed."

In their culture it was a serious thing not to return something you had borrowed, and although the reader is not told exactly what punishment the man anticipated for the loss of the axe head, he was obviously very concerned about it. However, we can assume that the reason for including the story in the scriptures at all is in what happened next.

Elisha stepped forward and asked the distraught man, "Where fell it?"

The worker immediately showed him the place where the axe head had entered the river. A "stick" was cut, and presumably it was Elisha who cast it into the river over the spot where the axe head had disappeared.

And that leads us to the rest of this amazing story:

1413. What did the axe head miraculously do when the "stick" was cast into the river? (2 Kings 6:6–7)

Searching
The Old
Testament

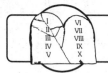
830. What did Saul do to Samuel's mantle as Samuel tried to leave? (1 Sam. 15:27)

831. How many times did the dove return to Noah's Ark? (Gen. 8:9–11)

832. What did Elisha provide for Jehoshaphat in the wilderness? (2 Kings 3:17, 20)

833. What is the last word of the book of Numbers?

834. What is the last word (thought to be a musical direction) of the third Psalm? (Ps. 3:8)

835. How many songs did Solomon write? (1 Kings 4:32)

836. Whose sword did David use to kill Goliath? (1 Sam. 17:51)

837. What was an Israelite called who vowed not to cut his hair or drink wine? (Num. 6:2–3, 5)

838. Queen Vashti was banished because she refused to come to the King when bidden. As a consequence, the king sent letters throughout his empire declaring that every man should bear rule in his own what? (Esther 1:12, 22)

839. What is the last book in the *Old Testament*?

840. How many books are in the *Old Testament*?

841. Who is generally credited with writing Ecclesiastes? (Eccl. 1:1)

842. In addition to the tithes what did the Levites receive as an inheritance in the promised land? (Joshua 21:41)

843. What book in the *Old Testament* describes the creation?

844. There are only two books in the *Old Testament* named after women: one is Esther, the other is what?

845. The children of Israel, at the time of Hezekiah, burned incense to Nehushtan in the groves. What was Nehushtan? (2 Kings 18:4)

846. Esther agreed to go before the king, "not according to the law." She told Mordecai, "if I _____, I _____." (Esther 4:16)

847. Deuteronomy is a record of the last words of what prophet to the children of Israel? (Deut. 1:1)

848. Who was Adam's "help meet"? (Gen. 2:20, 23)

849. Where did Mordecai sit each day? (Esther 2:21)

850. The Lord told Jeremiah, "many _____ have destroyed my vineyard, they have trodden My portion under foot." (Jer. 12:10)

TRUE OR FALSE

1375. One of the plagues Moses brought upon Pharaoh was to turn river water into blood when it was poured upon dry land. (Ex. 4:9)

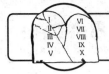
Match the questions on the left with the answers on the right. The solution is on page 273.

A. Who wrote the first five books in the *Old Testament*?

B. What is the last book in the *Old Testament*?

C. What is the first book in the *Old Testament*?

D. In Psalm 23, what did the Lord "restoreth" to David? (Ps. 23:3)

E. What book in the *Old Testament* describes the Israelites leaving Egypt?

F. What king's sons were killed before his eyes? (2 Kings 25:7)

G. The book of Lamentations is attributed to what prophet? (See Book Title)

H. What book and chapter contains Solomon's temple dedication prayer?

I. Who lived nine hundred and sixty-nine years? (Gen. 5:27)

J. Who was Amittai's famous "swallowed" son? (Jonah 1:1)

K. Generally speaking, the Psalms are credited to which king of Israel?

L. What book and chapter prophesies of John the Baptist?

M. Who is generally credited with writing the Proverbs? (Prov. 1:1)

N. Where is the book of Jehu? (2 Chron. 20:34)

Methuselah

Isaiah 40

Jonah

Solomon

Genesis

David

Lost

Exodus

Moses

Zedekiah

1 Kings 8

Jeremiah

His soul

Malachi

851. What book precedes Malachi?

852. What book precedes Haggai?

853. What book precedes Psalms?

854. What book precedes Isaiah?

855. What book precedes Joel?

856. What book precedes Leviticus?

857. What book precedes Jeremiah?

858. What book precedes 2 Chronicles?

859. What book precedes Hosea?

860. What book precedes Esther?

861. What book precedes 2 Kings?

862. What book precedes Ecclesiastes?

863. What book precedes Lamentations?

864. What book precedes Job?

865. What book precedes Deuteronomy?

866. What book precedes Zephaniah?

867. What book precedes Nahum?

868. What book precedes Proverbs?

869. What book precedes Ezekiel?

870. What book precedes Judges?

871. What book precedes Amos?

872. What book precedes Obadiah?

873. What book precedes Daniel?

874. What book precedes Numbers?

875. What book precedes Ezra?

876. What book precedes 2 Samuel?

877. What is the book that precedes Song of Solomon?

878. What book precedes Zechariah?

879. What book precedes Joshua?

880. What book precedes Ruth?

881. What book precedes Habakkuk?

882. What book precedes Nehemiah?

883. What book precedes 1 Chronicles?

884. What book precedes Micah?

885. What book precedes Jonah?

886. What book precedes 1 Kings?

887. What book precedes 1 Samuel?

888. What book precedes Exodus?

Solution on page 278

```
R  N  H  R  H  J  W  S  Q  H  B  F  W
I  X  V  E  J  N  R  A  Y  L  V  A  N
G  R  H  B  A  E  R  L  T  K  L  R  F
H  V  V  E  G  V  T  F  D  E  A  T  H
T  M  Y  N  R  H  E  L  L  K  R  F  M
E  C  I  T  H  I  Q  N  T  L  N  S  D
O  F  O  N  E  M  T  L  S  T  C  W  F
U  K  D  U  A  T  B  A  F  M  U  L  B
S  T  N  W  R  J  K  F  G  D  P  K  E
N  T  Q  T  T  A  A  F  L  E  N  N  R
E  N  V  R  B  T  G  D  A  Y  O  X  G
S  M  T  H  S  C  Y  E  T  T  K  L  P
S  L  E  A  R  T  H  K  S  N  N  T  H
```

- David said in Psalms that as he walked "though the valley of the shadow of death," God's rod and His _____ comforted him. (Ps. 23:4)

- In Psalm 23, David walked through the valley of the shadow of what? (Ps. 23:4)

- Psalm 127:3 declares that children are an _____ of the Lord.

- Psalm 19:8 declares that "The statutes of the Lord are right, rejoicing the" what?

- David recognized how small man was when he considered the "work" of God's what ? (Ps. 8:3)

- David declared in Psalms that God would not leave his soul in what undesirable place? (Ps. 16:10)

- In Psalms, David declared, the Lord "leadeth me beside the still" what? (Ps. 23:2)

- David declared in Psalms that his what "runneth over"? (Ps. 23:5)

- In Psalm 23:3, David declared, the Lord "leadeth me in the paths of" what? (Ps. 23:3)

- Psalm 118:22 declares that the _____ the builders refused would became the headstone of the corner.

- David declared in Psalm 24 that this orb is the Lord's, including the fullness thereof. (Ps. 24:1)

- In Psalm 19:1, David declares that the glory of God is made evident by the what? (Ps. 19:1)

- This Psalm declares that blessed is the man whose delight is in the what of the Lord? (Ps. 1:1–2)

- David stated in Psalm 7:11 that God judged the righteous, but was angry with the wicked every what?

- David instructs us in Psalms to be of "good" what, and wait upon the Lord? (Ps. 27:14)

TRICK QUESTION

1403. Who saw the angel in the path of Balaam's donkey? (Num. 22:23)

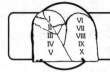
889. What book follows Isaiah?

890. What is the book that follows Song of Solomon?

891. What book follows 1 Kings?

892. What book follows 2 Chronicles?

893. What book follows Numbers?

894. What book follows Jeremiah?

895. What book follows Haggai?

896. What book follows Judges?

897. What book follows Hosea?

898. What book follows Ruth?

899. What book follows 1 Chronicles?

900. What book follows Job?

901. What book follows Genesis?

902. What book follows Ezekiel?

903. What book follows Nahum?

904. What book follows 2 Samuel?

905. What book follows Zechariah?

906. What book follows Proverbs?

907. What is the book after Deuteronomy?

908. What book follows Obadiah?

909. What book follows Exodus?

910. What book follows Jonah?

911. What book follows Daniel?

912. What book follows Joshua?

913. What book follows Ezra?

914. What book follows 1 Samuel?

915. What book follows Amos?

916. What book follows Esther?

917. What book follows Zephaniah?

918. What book follows 2 Kings?

919. What book follows Ecclesiastes?

920. What book follows Joel?

921. What book follows Leviticus?

922. What book follows Nehemiah?

923. What book follows Psalms?

924. What book follows Micah?

925. What book follows Lamentations?

926. What book follows Habakkuk?

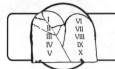

927. What is 1 Samuel "Otherwise Called"?

928. What is 2 Samuel "Otherwise called"?

929. What is the fourth book of Moses called?

930. What is the common name of The Fourth Book of the Kings?

931. What is the full name of Psalms?

932. What is the full name of Lamentations?

933. What book is known as The Preacher?

934. What is the name of the book wherein the people of Israel are counted?

935. What is the full name of 2 Kings?

936. What is the fifth book of Moses called?

937. What is the name of the lost book that records that the sun stood still while the people avenged themselves upon their enemies? (Joshua 10:13)

938. What is the more common name for "The Second Book of the Kings"?

939. What is the third book of Moses called?

940. What is the "commonly called" name of The First Book of the Kings?

941. What is the full title of 1 Samuel?

942. What is the full name of the book of 1 Kings?

943. What is the full name of 2 Samuel?

944. What is the common name of the book that is also named "The Third Book of the Kings"?

945. What is the second book of Moses called?

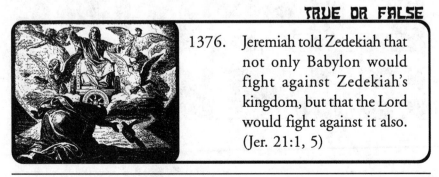

TRUE OR FALSE

1376. Jeremiah told Zedekiah that not only Babylon would fight against Zedekiah's kingdom, but that the Lord would fight against it also. (Jer. 21:1, 5)

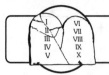
Solution on page 276

Across

1 "Trust in the Lord with all thine heart; and lean not unto thine own _____ ." (Prov. 3:5)

3 "For whom the Lord loveth he _____ ; even as a father the son in whom he delighteth." (Prov. 3:12)

8 "The fear of the Lord is the beginning of knowledge: but fools despise wisdom and _____ ." (Prov. 1:7)

10 The Lord hates a "_____ look." (Prov. 6:17)

12 "A word fitly spoken is like _____ of gold." (Prov. 25:11)

13 "_____ goeth before destruction, and an haughty spirit before a fall." (Prov. 16:18)

14 "I was set up from everlasting, from the beginning, or ever the _____ was." (Prov. 8:23)

16 "The glory of young men is their strength: and the _____ of old men is the gray head." (Prov. 20:29)

17 "He that hath no rule over his own spirit is like a city that is broken down, and without _____ ." (Prov. 25:28)

19 "For as he thinketh in his _____ , so is he." (Prov. 23:7)

20 "The fear of the Lord is the beginning of _____ : but fools despise wisdom and instruction." (Prov. 1:7)

21 "The way of a fool is right in his own eyes: but he that hearkeneth unto counsel is _____ ." (Prov. 12:15)

24 "Through _____ is an house builded; and by understanding it is established." (Prov. 24:3)

26 "Who can find a virtuous woman? for her price is far above _____ ." (Prov. 31:10)

30 "_____ up a child in the way he should go." (Prov. 22:6)

31 "He that is slow to _____ is better than the mighty." (Prov. 16:32)

32 "Pride goeth before destruction, and an haughty spirit before a _____ ." (Prov. 16:18)

33 "A soft _____ turneth away wrath." (Prov. 15:1)

36 "A foolish son is the heaviness of his _____ ." (Prov. 10:1)

40 "A froward man soweth _____ : and a whisperer separateth chief friends." (Prov. 16:28)

41 "A talebearer revealeth _____ , but he that is of a faithful spirit concealeth the matter." (Prov. 11:13)

42 "Thou shalt beat him (the child) with the rod, and shalt deliver his _____ from hell." (Prov. 23:14)

43 The Lord hates "he that soweth _____ among brethren." (Prov. 6:19)

45 "These six things doth the Lord hate: yea, _____ are an abomination unto him." (Prov. 6:16)

47 "Where there is no vision, the _____ perish." (Prov. 29:18)

50 "Where no counsel is, the people fall: but in the multitude of _____ there is safety." (Prov. 11:14)

52 "The _____ of man, is the candle of the Lord." (Prov. 20:27)

54 "_____ is a mocker, strong drink is raging: and whosoever is deceived thereby is not wise." (Prov. 20:1)

56 "He that regards reproof is _____ ." (Prov. 15:5)

59 "The way of a fool is right in his own eyes: but he that hearkeneth unto _____ is wise." (Prov. 12:15)

61 "Thou shalt beat him (the child) with a _____ , and shalt deliver his soul from hell." (Prov. 23:14)

62 "A talebearer revealeth secrets: but he that is of a faithful spirit _____ the matter." (Prov. 11:13)

64 The Lord hates "feet that be swift in running to _____ ." (Prov. 6:18)

65 "Train up a _____ in the way he should go: and when he is old, he will not depart from it." (Prov. 22:6)

66 "For whom the Lord _____ he correcteth." (Prov. 3:12)

Down

2 "A _____ answer turneth away wrath: but grievous words stir up anger." (Prov. 15:1)

4 "The spirit of man, is the _____ of the Lord." (Prov. 20:27)

5 "He that ruleth his spirit (is mightier) than he that taketh a _____." (Prov. 16:32)

6 "He that covereth a transgression seeketh _____." (Prov. 17:9)

7 "And by knowledge shall the chambers be filled with all precious and pleasant _____." (Prov. 24:4)

9 "A merry heart maketh a _____ countenance: but by sorrow of the heart the spirit is broken." (Prov. 15:13)

11 "The beauty of old men is their _____ head." (Prov. 20:29)

15 "A fool despiseth his _____ instruction: but he that regardeth reproof is prudent." (Prov. 15:5)

17 "Whoso findeth a _____ findeth a good thing, and obtaineth favour of the Lord." (Prov. 18:22)

18 "Wine is a _____, strong drink is raging: and whosoever is deceived thereby is not wise." (Prov. 20:1)

22 "The glory of young men is their _____." (Prov. 20:29)

23 "_____ is bound in the heart of a child; but the rod of correction shall drive it far from him." (Prov. 22:15)

25 "It is better to dwell in a corner of the housetop, than with a brawling _____ in a wide house." (Prov. 21:9)

27 "A _____ fitly spoken is like apples of gold in pictures of silver." (Prov. 25:11)

28 "Wine is a mocker, and strong _____ is raging." (Prov. 20:1)

29 The Lord hates "the hands that shed _____." (Prov. 6:17)

34 "How much better is it to get wisdom than gold! and to get understanding rather to be chosen than _____." (Prov. 16:16)

35 "Pride goeth before _____, and a haughty spirit before a fall." (Prov. 16:18)

37 "He that covereth a transgression seeketh love; but he that repeateth a matter separateth very _____." (Prov. 17:9)

38 "Where there is no _____, the people perish." (Prov. 29:18)

39 "It is better to dwell in the _____, than with a contentious and an angry woman." (Prov. 21:19)

44 "Through wisdom is an _____ builded; and by understanding it is established." (Prov. 24:3)

46 "Who can find a _____ woman? for her price is far above rubies." (Prov. 31:10)

48 "Where no wood is, there the fire goeth out: so where there is no talebearer, the strife _____." (Prov. 26:20)

49 One of the things the Lord hates is "a lying _____." (Prov. 6:17)

51 "These _____ things doth the Lord hate." (Prov. 6:16)

53 "Whoso loveth instruction loveth knowledge: but he that hateth _____ is brutish." (Prov. 12:1)

55 The Lord hates, "an heart that deviseth _____ imaginations." (Prov. 6:18)

57 "As a dog returneth to his _____, so a fool returneth to his folly." (Prov. 26:11)

58 "The way of the fool, is _____ in his own eyes." (Prov. 12:15)

60 "The _____ of the eyes rejoiceth the heart." (Prov. 15:30)

63 "Trust in the _____ with all thine heart; and lean not unto thine own understanding." (Prov. 3:5)

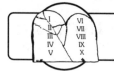
Match the questions on the left with the answers on the right. The solution is on page 271.

A. In Psalm 23, David said he would not fear this because God was with him. (Ps. 23:4)

Green

B. In Psalm 23, goodness and this divine attribute were to follow David all the days of his life. (Ps. 23:6)

Angels

C. In Psalm 23 it says the Lord "maketh" David to lie down in what color pastures? (Ps. 23:2)

God

D. In Psalms, David declares that man is a little lower than what heavenly beings? (Ps. 8:5)

Evil

E. The psalmist said that sinners will not stand in the congregation of what good people? (Ps. 1:5)

Peace

F. What Psalm was fulfilled when Jesus healed the nobleman's son by word only? (John 4:46–54)

The Righteous

G. Psalm 85:10 declares that righteousness and this calm attribute have "kissed" each other.

Psalm 107:20

H. According to Psalm 14:1, a fool says in his heart that this Deity does not exist.

Mercy

Challenged by the Old Testament

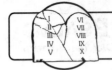
946. The Preacher declared that one generation passes away and another comes, but what abides forever? (Eccl. 1:4)

947. Isaiah teaches the doctrine of the "fast" in what chapter?

948. What is a "Chemarims," as noted in Zephaniah? (Zeph. 1:4)

949. According to the Preacher, for every purpose under heaven, there is a season and a what? (Eccl. 3:1)

950. The Preacher begins his "time to" sequence with: There is a time to be born, and a time to do what? (Eccl. 3:2)

951. According to the Preacher, he that increases knowledge, increases what? (Eccl. 1:18)

952. Jeremiah said that both _____ and priest were profane. (Jer. 23:11)

953. The Psalmist declared that the sinner would not stand in the congregation of the what? (Ps. 1:5)

954. According to the Preacher, there is no just man that doeth good, that does not do what? (Eccl. 7:20)

955. The Preacher declares over and over that all is what? (Eccl. 1:2)

956. According to the Preacher, the day of death is better than the day of what? (Eccl. 7:1)

957. The Preacher concluded that the whole duty of man is to fear God and keep what edicts? (Eccl. 12:13)

958. Jeremiah declared that both prophet and what were profane during his time? (Jer. 23:11)

959. What did the Preacher declare was better than precious ointment? (Eccl. 7:1)

960. According to Samuel, to obey is better than what? (1 Sam. 15:22)

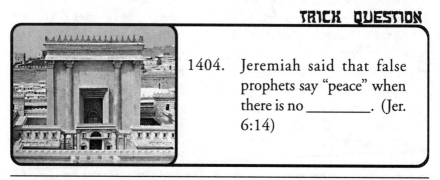

TRICK QUESTION

1404. Jeremiah said that false prophets say "peace" when there is no _____. (Jer. 6:14)

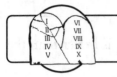
Solution on page 282

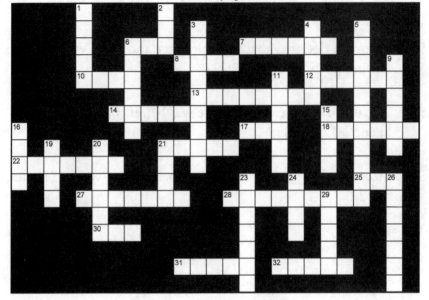

Across

6   Eve was called "woman" because she was taken out of whom? (Gen. 2:23)

7   What did the Lord tell every woman in Israel to do to the Egyptians when the Israelites left Egypt? (Ex. 3:22)

8   Ruth went to glean in the fields of Naomi's kinsman. What was his name? (Ruth 2:1)

10   Jezebel hated Elijah and threaten to do what to him? (1 Kings 19:1–2)

12   The servant of which prophet requested that a Shunammite woman be blessed with a son. (2 Kings 4:8, 14)

13   What was Hagar's nationality? (Gen. 16:1)

14   Queen Vashti, displeased the king by refusing to come when what? (Esther 1:12)

17   The name of the person God created from Adam's rib. (Gen. 2:21–22)

18   Who replaced Vashti as King Ahasuerus' queen? (Esther 2:17)

21   "It is better to dwell in the wilderness, than with a contentious and angry" what? (Prov. 21:19)

22   What Shunammite woman did Adonijah desire to have as a wife after Solomon became king? (1 Kings 2:17)

25 Two women bargained to do this cannibalistic thing to each other's sons during a great famine. The story caused their king to rend his clothes. (2 Kings 6:28)

27 What did Ruth do in the fields of Boaz? (Ruth 2:2)

28 Vashti was queen to what king? (Esther 1:9)

30 How many books in the *Old Testament* are named after women?

31 Deborah was the first woman in Israel to serve in this position. (Judges 4:4)

32 What was the name of the Midianite woman who was slain with Zimri by Phinehas? (Num. 25:15)

Down

1 When Eli first saw Hannah praying (her lips moving soundlessly), he thought she was what? (1 Sam. 1:14)

2 According to the Law of Moses, a daughter could inherit from her father when there was no what? (Num. 27:8)

3 Hosea was commanded to take a wife from the women of what unsavory profession? (Hosea. 1:2)

4 Proverb 31 extols the praises of what sex?

5 Ezekiel likened Israel and Judah to two daughters of what profession? (Ezek. 23)

6 Who was Nehor's wife? (Gen. 11:29)

9 Saul sought the witch of Endor so that she could conjure up this prophet for him. (1 Sam. 28:7, 11)

11 How old was Sarah when Isaac was born? (Gen. 17:17)

15 As Boaz slept, Ruth uncovered his _____ and slept by them. (Ruth 3:7)

16 The "wise woman of Abel," to preserve her city, cut off what part of a traitor's body? (2 Sam. 20:18, 22)

19 In the story of the creation, Eve was created from one of these. (It came from Adam.) (Gen. 2:21–22)

20 What was Rahab's profession? (Joshua 2:1)

21 In Jeremiah, the Lord compares Israel to an unfaithful what? (Jer. 3:1, 8)

23 The Shunammite woman provided a _____ for Elisha when he traveled. (2 Kings 4:10)

24 Naomi had two daughters-in-law. Which one stayed with her? (Ruth 1:14–15)

26 Hannah vowed that if she conceived a male child, she would give him to whom? (1 Sam. 1:11)

29 What is the name of the harlot who assisted Israel's spies in Jericho? (Joshua 2:1)

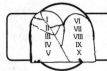

961. What happened to the shoes and clothes of the Israelites during their wilderness trek? (Deut. 29:5)

962. What did Adam and Eve make out of fig leaves in the Garden? (Gen. 3:7)

963. What clothing did Isaiah have on when he walked for three years as a sign to Egypt and Ethiopia? (Is. 20:2–3)

964. Of what did the Lord God make Adam and Eve's first clothes? (Gen. 3:21)

965. Moses was commanded to make holy garments for whom? (Ex. 28:2)

966. The girdle Elijah had around his loins was made of what? (2 Kings 1:8)

967. What should men and women NOT wear according to the Law of Moses? (Deut. 22:5)

968. What color was the garment of the "Ancient of days" when he appeared to Daniel? (Dan. 7:9)

969. To prepare themselves to see God, the Israelites were to sanctify themselves and wash their what? (Ex. 19:10–11)

970. To prove that he was loyal to Saul, David cut off the skirt of Saul's what, as he slept? (1 Sam. 24:4)

971. After Jonah's warning of destruction, the king of Nineveh put on what? (Jonah 3:6)

972. Moses was told by the Lord to put off his shoes, for he was standing on what type of ground? (Ex. 3:5)

TRUE OR FALSE

1377. The disobedient man of God in First Kings was slain by a lion. (1 Kings 13:26)

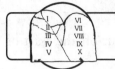
973. What color was Esau when he was born? (Gen. 25:25)

974. Upon what substance were the ten commandments written? (Ex. 24:12)

975. A Nazarite would vow not to cut his what? (Num. 6:5)

976. Jeremiah declared the unique "breaking" of northern iron and what other metal? (Jer. 15:12)

977. What building did the "adversaries" of Judah and Benjamin ask Zerubabel to help them build? (Ezra 4:1–2)

978. What was the penalty for failure to worship the golden image King Nebuchadnezzar had set up? (Dan. 3:6)

979. What is the unique word used to describe the gifts offered to Elisha by Naaman because Naaman had been healed of leprosy? (2 Kings 5:15–16)

980. The woman of Endor conjured up Samuel at whose request? (1 Sam. 28:7, 11)

981. When Elisha told him how to be healed of leprosy, Naaman's first reaction was to become _____. (2 Kings 5:11)

982. Who took Ezekiel "up" so that he could see his vision? (Ezek. 3:12)

983. What happened to the first captain and fifty sent by King Ahab to capture Elijah? (2 Kings 1:10)

984. Abimelech asked his servant to kill him to avoid being killed by a what? (Judges 9:54)

985. Who did Nehemiah consult when he rebuked the nobles and rulers? (Neh. 5:7)

986. The Lord commanded Jeremiah NOT to do what for the people? (Jer. 11:14)

987. How was Sisera killed? (Judges 4:21)

988. What unique physical features did the giant killed by Jonathan have? (2 Sam. 21:20)

989. How did the Lord plan to transport Elijah up into heaven? (2 Kings 2:1)

990. Who did the flames from the fiery furnace slay according to the book Daniel? (Dan. 3:22)

991. Who caused an axe head to swim? (2 Kings 6:1–6)

992. What did Isaiah say was the answer of the learned man who was asked to read a sealed book? (Is. 29:11)

993. Although he was from the tribe of Benjamin, Mordecai was called by what nationality? (Esther 2:5)

994. What vehicle appeared to receive Elijah into heaven? (2 Kings 2:11)

995. Who shut Noah into the Ark? (Gen. 7:16)

996. A Nazarite commonly abstained from eating unclean things. What are two other things that were required of him? (Judges 13:4–5)

MATCHES ABOUT MOTHERS
Searching The Old Testament

Match the questions on the left with the answers on the right. The solution is on page 269.

A. Who was the great-grandmother of David? She was a Moabite. (Ruth 4:13, 22)

Eve

B. What relation was the mother of the children of Moab to Lot? (Gen. 19:36–37)

Ruth

C. Ruth was the great-grandmother of which Israelite king? (Ruth 4:13–22)

Hannah

D. Who was Samuel's mother? (1 Sam. 1:20)

His older daughter

E. Who is the mother of all living? (Gen. 3:20)

His younger daughter

F. Who is the mother of Lot? (Gen. 11:27, 31)

David

G. Who was promised to be the mother of nations? (Gen. 17:15–16)

Unknown

H. What relation was the mother of the children of Ammon to Lot? (Gen. 19:36, 38)

Sarah

Dreams And
Visions

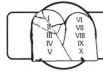

IX

THE MAN-IMAGE DREAM
Dreams And Visions

997. The feet of the man-image in Nebuchadnezzar's dream were made of what? (Dan. 2:33)

998. The belly and thighs of the man-image in Nebuchadnezzar's dream were made of what? (Dan. 2:32)

999. The head of the man-image in Nebuchadnezzar's dream was made of what metal? (Dan. 2:32)

1000. Nebuchadnezzar beheld a great image in his dream that he could not remember, and the form thereof was _____. (Dan. 2:31)

1001. The legs of the man-image in Nebuchadnezzar's dream were made of what metal? (Dan. 2:33)

1002. The breast and arms of the man-image in Nebuchadnezzar's dream were made of what metal? (Dan. 2:32)

TRICK QUESTION

1405. In 1 Samuel, who does it say slew Saul? (1 Sam. 31:4)

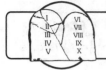

Solution on page 260

Across

1 Who revealed the forgotten dream of Nebuchadnezzar to Daniel? (Dan. 2:28)

4 The one notable horn of the he goat in Daniel's vision was located between his what? (Dan. 8:5)

5 Daniel was protected in the lion's den by one of these heavenly beings. (Dan. 6:22)

8 What city did Daniel face when he prayed? (Dan. 6:10)

9 Daniel was a captive from which tribe of Israel? (Dan. 2:25)

11 How many times each day did Daniel pray? (Dan. 6:10)

15 In Daniel's vision, the Son of man comes to the Ancient of what? (Dan. 7:13)

16 God gave Daniel an understanding of dreams and _____ . (Dan. 1:17)

20 The wicked cannot understand Daniel's prophesies, but the _____ can. (Dan. 12:10)

21 Which of the four beasts in Daniel's vision had wings like an eagle? (Dan. 7:4)

22 In the handwriting on the wall, Daniel interpreted the word "TEKEL" to mean Belshazzar was found what? (Dan. 5:27)

25 Before the little horn of Daniel's vision rose among them, three of the first horns were plucked up by the what? (Dan. 7:8)

27 What did the king do while Daniel was in the lion's den? (Dan. 6:18)

30 What was Daniel's Chaldean name? (Dan. 1:7)

32 How many horns did the he goat in Daniel's vision have? (Dan. 8:5)

33 Nebuchadnezzar had forgotten his _____ , but Daniel was able to remember it. (Dan. 2:5)

34 In Daniel's vision of a man, the man's face was described as being like what? (Dan. 10:6)

Down

1 The ram in Daniel's vision was destroyed by the "he _____ ." (Dan. 8:5, 7)

2 Rather than the king's meat, what food did Daniel request? (Dan. 1:12)

3 How many weeks are symbolically numbered as time periods in the visions of Daniel? (Dan. 9:24)

6 In his vision, the animal that Daniel saw by the river was a what? (Dan. 8:3)

7 After Daniel escaped unharmed, the king put Daniel's accusers in the lion's what? (Dan. 6:24)

10 Daniel was cast into the lion's den for breaking the decree of what king? (Dan. 6:9, 16)

12 Who was the king displeased with when he had to punish Daniel? (Dan. 6:14)

13 Daniel was instructed to seal the book he envisioned until the time of the what? (Dan. 12:4)

14 In Daniel's vision, what are opened at the final judgment? (Dan. 7:10)

17 The fourth beast of Daniel's vision had how many horns on its head? (Dan. 7:19–20)

18 In the story of the fiery furnace found in the book of Daniel, how many men were seen in the furnace? (Dan. 3:25)

19 The four beasts in Daniel's vision represent four what? (Dan. 7:17)

20 What would Daniel NOT drink? (Dan. 1:8)

22 What did Daniel want to drink in place of the king's wine? (Dan. 1:12)

23 Who did the king say would deliver Daniel from the lion's den? (Dan. 6:16)

24 Belshazzar was told about Daniel's abilities by his _____ . (Dan. 5:10–11, 13)

26 What was the name of the angel that touched Daniel while he was praying? (Dan. 9:21)

28 Who brought Daniel before king Nebuchadnezzar and told him that Daniel could interpret the king's dream? (Dan. 2:25)

29 How many horns did the ram in Daniel's vision have? (Dan. 8:3)

31 A little _____ came up among the ten horns in Daniel's vision. (Dan. 7:8)

35 Could the leaders find any error or fault in Daniel? (Dan. 6:4)

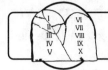
1003. Joseph interpreted dreams for these two servants of Pharaoh. (Gen. 40:2)

1004. What did Jacob see in his dream that began on the earth and extended into heaven? (Gen. 28:12)

1005. Which of Pharaoh's servants was restored to his position in a dream revealed to Joseph? (Gen. 40:9–13)

1006. What did Nebuchadnezzar do after Daniel revealed his forgotten dream to him? (Dan. 2:46)

1007. What did the tree in Nebuchadnezzar's dream represent? (Dan. 4:22)

1008. What problem did Nebuchadnezzar have with his dream? (Dan. 2:5)

1009. What name did Jacob give the place where he had his dream of a ladder? (Gen. 28:19)

1010. In Nebuchadnezzar's dream, what did he see in the midst of the earth? (Dan. 4:10)

1011. Which of Pharaoh's servants was killed in the dream that was revealed to Joseph? (Gen. 40:16–19)

1012. Which of Jacob's sons interpreted Pharaoh's dreams? (Gen. 41:25)

1013. Who appeared to Solomon in a dream at Gibeon? (1 Kings 3:5)

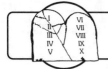

DANIEL AND HIS VISION
Dreams And Visions

Match the questions on the left with the answers on the right. The solution is on page 260.

A. Daniel met with Nebuchadnezzar because of what order? (Dan. 2:13–16)

B. How long did Daniel stay in the lion's den? (Dan. 6:18–19)

C. In Daniel, what is "set up" at the conclusion of 1290 days? (Dan. 12:11)

D. Which animal had only one notable horn in Daniel's vision, the ram or the he goat? (Dan. 8:5)

E. What two kingdoms were represented by two horns of a ram in Daniel's vision? (Dan. 8:20)

F. The four beasts of Daniel's vision were like a lion, a bear, a leopard, and a what? (Dan. 7:4–7)

G. In Daniel's vision, how long would the daily sacrifice cease? (Dan. 8:14)

H. What did the ten horns in the beast of Daniel's vision represent? (Dan. 7:24)

I. In Daniel's vision, what part of a beast symbolically made war with the saints? (Dan. 7:8, 21)

J. How long was it between the end of sacrifice and the beginning of the abomination of desolation spoken of by Daniel? (Dan. 12:11)

K. Who came to the "Ancient of days" in Daniel's vision? (Dan. 7:13)

L. Who was instructed to explain Daniel's vision of a ram to him? (Dan. 8:16)

M. Who revealed Nebuchadnezzar's forgotten dream to Daniel? (Dan. 2:28)

Ten kings

Gabriel

One like the Son of man

Overnight

God

A little horn

Media and Persia

Two thousand three hundred days

The abomination of desolation

Destroy all the wise men

Twelve hundred and ninety days

Beast with ten horns.

The he goat

1014. What were the four faces of the creatures in Ezekiel's first vision? (Ezek. 1:10)

1015. In the vision of Zechariah, what was the color of the horses in the first chariot? (Zech. 6:2)

1016. Who was the fourth man that Nebuchadnezzar saw in the fiery furnace? (Dan. 3:25)

1017. What was represented by the flying "roll," in the vision of Zechariah? (Zech. 5:3)

1018. What were the two olive branches defined as in the vision of Zechariah? (Zech. 4:14)

1019. The boy Samuel feared to show his first vision to whom? (1 Sam. 3:15)

1020. What did the four horses in Zechariah's vision represent? (Zech. 6:5)

1021. What word does Habakkuk use to describe his vision in Habakkuk 1:1?

1022. Ezekiel began his first vision when he saw what weather phenomenon coming out of the north? (Ezek. 1:4)

1023. Who appeared to Lot in Sodom and warned him to leave? (Gen. 19:1)

1024. What did Elisha's servant see a mountain full of when God opened his eyes? (2 Kings 6:17)

1025. What did Moses see in vision just prior to his death? (Num. 27:12)

1026. In the vision of Zechariah, what was the color of the horses pulling the third chariot? (Zech. 6:3)

1027. In Ezekiel's first vision he saw a whirlwind, a cloud, and a what? (Ezek. 1:4)

1028. How many wings did the seraphim have that Isaiah saw in his vision? (Is. 6:2)

TRICK QUESTION

1406. Who did Elisha instruct the king to send Naaman to see? (2 Kings 5:8)

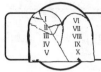

SYMBOLISM CROSSWORD
Dreams And Visions

Solution on page 281

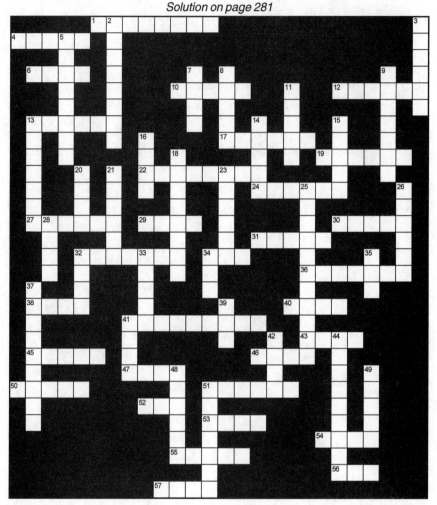

Across

1 God made Ezekiel what type of guard unto the house of Israel? (Ezek. 3:17)

4 What appendages were under the wings of the creatures Ezekiel saw in his vision? (Ezek. 1:8)

6 How many faces did the creatures of Ezekiel's vision have? (Ezek. 1:6)

10 Ezekiel was commanded to write upon two "sticks": one was for Ephraim and the other for whom? (Ezek. 37:16)

12 What fell from Elijah as he was taken into heaven? (2 Kings 2:13)

13 In symbolic prophecy, the Lord told Zechariah to cast thirty pieces of sil-

ver to what type of artisan? (Zech. 11:13)

17 In poetic prophecy, Isaiah said that the vision of "all is become unto you as the words of a book" that is in what condition? (Is. 29:11)

19 Jeremiah hid this linen clothing article in a hole in a rock to witness against Judah's pride. (Jer. 13:4)

22 How much of Ezekiel's cut hair was he to chop with a knife? (Ezek. 5:2)

24 Isaiah said that Ariel would be brought down low and that its speech would be as one with a familiar what? (Is. 29:4)

27 In 1 Kings, how many oxen supported the "molten sea" of the temple? (1 Kings 7:25)

29 The soles of the feet of the creatures Ezekiel saw in vision looked like the soles of what calve's appendage? (Ezek. 1:7)

30 What servant of Pharaoh's (that prepared his food) was killed in the dream that was revealed to Joseph? (Gen. 40:16–19)

31 In poetic prophecy, Isaiah states that in the last days if you have clothing, people will want you to be what kind of leader? (Is. 3:6)

32 In symbolic verse concerning the gathering of the Israelites, Jeremiah declared that the Lord would send for many men of what profession to "fish" them? (Jer. 16:16)

34 In the description of Isaiah's Seraphim, two wings covered its face, two wings covered its feet, and with two wings it could perform what aerial activity? (Is. 6:2)

36 After Hananiah removed the yoke

from Jeremiah, what did he do with it? (Jer. 28:10)

38 What were in the rings of the wheel that Ezekiel saw? (Ezek. 1:18)

40 Ezekiel was commanded to set a _____ upon the foreheads of certain men in Jerusalem. (Ezek. 9:4)

41 What were the twelve loaves of bread in the tabernacle called? (Ex. 25:30; Lev. 24:5)

43 What item made of gold did Moses burn when he came down from Sinai? (Ex. 32:20)

45 As a witness of Israel's covenant with God, Joshua set what hard item before Israel? (Joshua 24:27)

46 Balaam said that even if Balak would give him silver and gold he could not go beyond the word of the Lord, less or _____ . (Num. 22:18)

47 Amos warned, "Woe to them that are at 'what' in Zion"? (Amos 6:1)

50 Isaiah declared that the Lord had poured out the spirit of what deep nocturnal condition? (Is. 29:10)

51 In poetic imagery, Isaiah says that the heavens "shall be rolled together as a" what? (Is. 34:4)

52 How many "sticks" was Ezekiel instructed by the Lord to write upon? (Ezek. 37:16)

53 In poetic prophecy, Isaiah said that the desert would blossom as a what? (Is. 35:1)

54 According to Isaiah, what must you be weaned from in order to understand doctrine? (Is. 28:9)

55 What did the roll taste like that Ezekiel ate? (Ezek. 3:3)

56 The Psalmist declared that his soul

thirsted for what living Deity? (Ps. 42:2)

57 In Deuteronomy, the Lord is described as what consuming element? (Deut. 4:24)

Down

2 Symbolically speaking, the Lord put the kingdom of Israel away for commiting what sin, yet her treacherous sister Judah went ahead and played the harlot? (Jer. 3:8)

3 Isaiah describes the future work that God will do among his people as a marvelous work and a what? (Is. 29:14)

5 Malachi declared that Judah had married what relation of a strange god? (Mal. 2:11)

7 In poetic prophecy, Isaiah declared that the words of Ariel (or Jerusalem) would speak out of the ground and low out of the what substance? (Is. 29:4)

8 What food made out of barley did Ezekiel eat as a sign to Israel? (Ezek. 4:12)

9 Obadiah prophesied that the house of Jacob would be a fire, the house of Joseph would be a flame, and the house of Esau would be for what? (Obad. 1:18)

11 Jacob symbolically blessed Dan to be like a "serpent by the way." What kind of serpent was he referring to? (Gen. 49:17)

13 The Lord put Moses in the position of a god to Pharaoh, and Moses' brother Aaron functioned as what type of seer? (Ex. 7:1)

14 Zechariah took up two staves. He named one Beauty and he named the other something that sounds like "sands." (Zech. 11:7)

15 Isaiah said to wait upon the Lord, and walk and not what? (Is. 40:31)

16 The Lord declared to Isaiah, "Though your sins be as scarlet, they shall be as white as" this type of precipitation. (Is. 1:18)

18 Zephaniah said because of the Lord's wrath, the land is devoured by the fire of the Lord's what? (Zeph. 1:18)

20 The seraphim purged Isaiah's sins with this live item found in a fire. (Is. 6:6-7)

21 What beings were ascending and descending Jacob's ladder? (Gen. 28:12)

23 Isaiah states that the vineyard of the Lord is the house of what people? (Is. 5:7)

25 A book of what type was written before God, "for them that feared the Lord, and that thought upon his name." (Mal. 3:16)

26 In vivid symbolism, the Lord told Jeremiah that He had "put away" Israel for her adultery, but her sister Judah had also played the what? (Jer. 3:8)

28 Isaiah states in poetic prophecy that even though you care for the vineyard, sometimes it brings forth what kind of grapes? (Is. 5:2)

32 In Jeremiah, the Lord describes two groups of captives from the people of Judah as baskets of what fruit? (Jer. 24:1)

33 Jacob's ladder was set up on what planet, (and it reached to heaven)? (Gen. 28:12)

34 In symbolic verse, Micah prophesied that after the Second Coming, every man would sit under what type of tree? (Micah 4:4)

35 Isaiah said the wicked are like this body of water when it is troubled. (Is. 57:20)

37 Zechariah envisioned a man with a measuring line. What city was the man going to measure? (Zech. 2:2)

39 Symbolically speaking, does Genesis describe the serpent as being more subtle than all the beasts of the field? (Gen. 3:1)

41 The sign of giving up redemption rights in the story of Ruth was that a man plucked off this foot covering, and gave it to his neighbor. (Ruth 4:7)

42 Ezekiel was commanded to eat what? (Ezek. 3:1)

44 The creatures of Ezekiel's vision left and then returned like what flash of light in the sky? (Ezek. 1:14)

48 Isaiah declared that the watchmen of Israel were greedy dogs, never having what? (Is. 56:11)

49 Ezekiel gave warning to the shepherds of Israel because they did not feed the _____ . (Ezek. 34:3)

51 In symbolic verse, Malachi declared that Judah had married the daughter of what type of god? (Mal. 2:11)

TRUE OR FALSE

1378. Jeremiah made bonds and chains and put them on his neck as a means of revealing God's intentions for Israel. (Jer. 27:2)

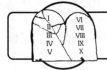
1029. Elijah called Elisha to succeed him by casting his what, upon him? (1 Kings 19:19)

1030. How many of Jezebel's "prophets of the groves" did Elijah bring to Carmel? (1 Kings 18:19)

1031. Elijah called down fire from heaven to consume how many captains and their fifty that had been sent by Ahab to capture him? (2 Kings 1:10, 12)

1032. How many prophets of Baal did Elijah command be gathered to him at Carmel? (1 Kings 18:19)

1033. What did Elijah do to the prophets of Baal? (1 Kings 18:40)

1034. What did Elijah tell Ahab would come only according to his word? (1 Kings 17:1)

1035. Which chapter in 1 Kings introduces Elijah to Israel?

1036. How did the widow of Zarephath know that Elisha was a man of God? (1 Kings 17:22–24)

1037. How is Elijah described? (2 Kings 1:8)

1038. What did the third captain of fifty do when he met Elijah? (2 Kings 1:13)

1039. Who fed Elijah before his trip to Horeb? (1 Kings 19:7–8)

1040. What holiday feast was held fifty days after Passover? (Ex. 23:16; Lev. 23:16; Deut. 16:10)

1041. What did Elijah prophesy concerning Ahab's death? (1 Kings 21:19)

1042. In which chapter in 1 Kings does Elijah raise the widow's son?

1379. Moses cast his rod into the bitter waters to heal them. (Ex. 15:25)

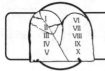

IMAGERY CROSSWORD
Dreams And Visions

Solution on page 265

Across

2 David commanded that a cruse of water and this weapon of Saul's be taken from him while he was sleeping so that David could prove his loyalty to Saul. (1 Sam. 26:11)

6 Who broke the yoke from Jeremiah's neck? (Jer. 28:10)

8 The Lord commanded Ezekiel to lie on his left side for three hundred and ninety days to signify the period of time Ezekiel would bear the people's what? (Ezek. 4:4)

9 When Jeremiah removed his hidden girdle (which represented a witness of Judah's pride), it was _____. (Jer. 13:7)

11 This is what Gideon made from golden earrings. (Judges 8:27)

14 Nebuchadnezzar ordered that everyone should fall down and do this to his statue. (Dan. 3:6)

15 In poetic prophecy, whose name was called "Wonderful" by Isaiah? (Is. 9:6)

17 Which appendages of the men in Ezekiel's vision sparkled like burnished brass? (Ezek. 1:7)

18 In Deuteronomy, the Lord is described as what kind of God? (Deut. 4:24)

20 The seraphim touched Isaiah's lips with a live coal to purge his what? (Is. 6:6–7)

23 At first, God commanded Ezekiel to bake his barley cakes with man's what? (Ezek. 4:12)

25 Zechariah said the people had made their _____ like an adamant stone. (Zech. 7:12)

29 The Lord manifested His acceptance of the tabernacle with a cloud and His what? (Ex. 40:34)

31 Twelve stones were taken from the river Jordan to commemorate Israel's what? (Joshua 4:3, 17)

32 In whose image was man made? (Gen. 1:27)

34 Michal, David's wife, was offended when David did this in front of all Israel. (2 Sam. 6:16)

36 Zechariah gave his two staves the names of Beauty and what? (Zech. 11:7)

37 Isaiah declared that those who would come of Jacob would take what, and afterward bud and produce fruit? (Is. 27:6)

Down

1 God's glory appeared to Ezekiel as what colorful phenomenon on a rainy day? (Ezek. 1:28)

2 In Jeremiah, the Lord said "woe be unto the pastors" that scatter My what? (Jer. 23:1)

3 Moses put the blood of the ram of consecration on Aaron's ear, thumb and foot. Were these on the left side or right side of his body? (Lev. 8:23)

4 Ezekiel was to join the two symbolic sticks spoken of in verse 18 down into one what? (Ezek. 37:17)

5 When the children's teeth are on edge, sour grapes have been eaten by the what? (Ezek. 18:2)

7 Ezekiel delivered a riddle in the form of a parable about two eagles and a what? (Ezek. 17)

10 What smote the man-image of Nebuchadnezzar's dream on the feet and broke them to pieces? (Dan. 2:34)

12 One-third of Ezekiel's cut hair was to be scattered in the what? (Ezek. 5:2)

13 Moses made a serpent of what metal to heal the Israelites from the bites of the "fiery serpents"? (Num. 21:9)

16 Isaiah declared that God had instituted this procedure to loose the bands of wickedness. (Is. 58:6)

18 Two tribes of Israel were represented by Ezekiel's sticks. One was Ephraim, the other was what? (Ezek. 37:16)

19 What cherubim's appendages covered the Ark of the Covenant when the priests put the Ark in the "holy place"? (1 Kings 8:6–7)

21 According to Obadiah, Jacob is the fire, Joseph the flame, and Esau is what residue? (Ob. 1:18)

22 Jacob made the coat of many colors for whom? (Gen. 37:3)

24 Psalm 19:8 declares that the commandments of the Lord are pure, enlightening what orbs?

26 Using poetic imagery, Isaiah said that God would lift up a what to the nations? (Is. 5:26)

27 Written on the forehead band of the crown worn by Aaron were the words, "Holiness to the _____." (Ex. 39:30)

28 The firstborn male in Israel was dedicated to the Lord to commemorate the Exodus from what country? (Num. 3:13)

30 What was used as a test to cease the murmuring of the other tribes in Israel against Moses and Aaron? (Aaron's budded.) (Num. 17:6–8)

33 In poetic imagery, Isaiah describes the nations as a _____ in a bucket. (Is. 40:15)

35 What did Israel have to do to the brass serpent to be healed from the bite of the "fiery serpents"? (Num. 21:9)

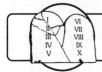
1043. What two prophets said that the house of the Lord would be established in the top of the mountains?

1044. Samuel, after he was presented to the Lord, was placed into the care of whom? (1 Sam 2:11)

1045. Who prophesied of Hananiah the prophet's death? (Jer. 28:15–16)

1046. How many prophets of the Lord did Elijah claim existed as he confronted the prophets of Baal? (1 Kings 18:22)

1047. Who did the Lord send to David after Uriah's death? (2 Sam. 12:1)

1048. What famous prophet lived during King Ahab's time (the Jews set an extra place for him at Passover)? (1 Kings 17:1)

1049. Amos prophesied that people would wander and seek, but would not find the word of whom? (Amos 8:12)

1050. Isaiah served as prophet during the reign of how many kings of Judah? (Is. 1:1)

1051. Which prophet did the Lord send to reproach David concerning his sins with Uriah and Bathsheba? (2 Sam. 12:1)

1052. Who anointed Elisha to be the next prophet? (1 Kings 19:16)

1053. What sign did Elisha see to verify his call to be the prophet after Elijah? (2 Kings 2:11, 14)

1054. What prophet was called a "Tishbite"? (1 Kings 17:1)

1055. Who knew that Samuel had been called to be a prophet? (1 Sam. 3:20)

1056. What was Elijah's first prophecy to Ahab? (1 Kings 17:1)

1057. What did God deny Jeremiah? (Jer. 16:2)

1058. Was Hananiah a false prophet or a true one? (Jer. 28:15)

1059. Baruch was a scribe to what prophet?

1060. Amos said the Lord would sift Israel among all _____. (Amos 9:9)

1061. Where is the book of Shemaiah the prophet? (2 Chron. 12:15)

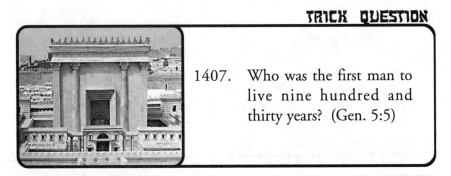

TRICK QUESTION

1407. Who was the first man to live nine hundred and thirty years? (Gen. 5:5)

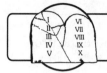

Solution on page 275

Across

1 To save their lives, who hid one hundred prophets from king Ahab? (1 Kings 18:4)

4 Who did Nehemiah consult before he rebuked the Jewish nobles and rulers? (Neh. 5:7)

5 Who perceived that it was God calling the boy Samuel? (1 Sam. 3:8)

7 Isaiah recorded that the people wanted the prophets to prophesy unto them not rough things, but things that were the opposite of rough. (Is. 30:10)

8 Isaiah was told to prophesy that the people would indeed hear, but would not what? (Is. 6:9)

9 Isaiah declared that future people

will want prophets to prophesy what misconceptions? (Is. 30:10)

10 What did Moses prophesy the Lord would raise up in the future that would be like unto himself? (Deut. 18:15)

12 Which prophet was a Morashthite? (Micah 1:1)

14 In poetic verse, Isaiah said that Jesus would be a man of sorrows and acquainted with what emotion? (Is. 53:3)

18 Zephaniah prophesied in the days of what king of Judah? (Zeph. 1:1)

20 Haggai's prophecy (generally speaking) concerns the construction of what building? (Haggai 1:8)

21 Which prophet was an Elkoshite by nationality? (Nahum 1:1)

23 Jeremiah said that God had not spoken to the prophets, yet they did this. (Jer. 23:21)

24 Which prophet was put in the stocks at the house of the Lord by the chief governor? (Jer. 20:2)

28 This man was the prophet at David's time. (2 Sam. 7:2)

30 What nationality was the prophet Nahum? (Nahum 1:1)

32 Ahijah prophesied that Jeroboam would reign over how many tribes of Israel? (1 Kings 11:30–31)

35 Gad the prophet was David's what? (2 Sam. 24:11)

36 When Nebuzaradan set Jeremiah free, where did he say he could go? (Jer. 40:1, 4)

38 Micah prophesied that a man's enemies would be of his own what? (Micah 7:6)

39 Where is the book of Nathan the prophet? (1 Chron. 29:29)

40 Which of the prophets is described as a "ready scribe"? (Ezra 7:6)

43 Who was the prophet that was Zechariah's grandfather? (Zech. 1:1)

44 Jeremiah told Zedekiah that he would be delivered into the hands of the king of what country? (Jer. 37:17)

45 To fulfil Elijah's prophecy, Ahab's blood was licked up by the dogs from the pool in which this type of vehicle was washed. (1 Kings 22:38)

46 When the Lord first spoke to Jeremiah, Jeremiah responded by saying that he could not speak because he was a what? (Jer. 1:6)

47 Prophesying of the future, Isaiah said people would travel so speedily that the latchet of what foot coverings would not be broken? (Is. 5:27)

Down

1 In poetic prophecy, Isaiah declared that one thousand would flee at the rebuke of how many? (Is. 30:17)

2 In poetic prophecy, Isaiah spoke of John the Baptist as a voice crying in what rural place? (Is. 40:3)

3 Micah prophesied that Zion would be what, as a field? (Micah 3:12)

6 What prophet did King Hezekiah seek for advice? (2 Kings 19:2)

11 This is another adjective describing how the Kingdom of Israel would be dispersed among the nations according to Ahijah's prophecy. (1 Kings 14:15)

13 Jeremiah declared that those who claimed to be prophets and were not, prophesied in this manner. (Jer. 5:31)

15 Ezekiel prophesied of two "sticks": one was from Judah the other from whom? (Ezek. 37:16)

16 Prophesying of the future, Isaiah said that the horses' hoofs would be counted like flint, and their wheels like what strong wind? (Is. 5:28)

17 What prophet was a cupbearer to King Artaxerxes? (Neh. 1:1, 11)

19 Jeremiah prophesied that Judah would be carried away in this restricted condition. (Jer. 13:19)

22 Amos prophesied that God would send a _____ in the land, not of food and drink, but of hearing the words of the Lord. (Amos 8:11)

25 What *Old Testament* prophet states that the sons of Levi will yet make an offering to the Lord in righteousness? (Malachi 3:3)

26 Isaiah prophesied that the Lord would lift up an ensign to the what? (Is. 5:26)

27 Who did God tell Ezekiel would be responsible for the"blood" of the wicked if he did not warn them of their wickedness? (Ezek. 3:18)

29 Jehudi burned the document that contained Jeremiah's prophecy. The document was called a what? (Jer. 36:23)

31 Who did Elijah anoint to be a prophet in his stead? (1 Kings 19:16)

32 Elijah was an inhabitant of Gilead, but was called Elijah the what? (1 Kings 17:1)

33 This is what Jeremiah prophesied false prophets would receive. (Jer. 14:15)

34 Jeremiah came from what community? (Jer. 1:1)

37 Which prophet held his famous contest between the gods on Mt. Carmel? (1 Kings 18:19, 21)

41 At his contest between the gods, Elijah mocked the prophets of whom? (1 Kings 18:19, 27)

42 What did Ezekiel say fathers would eat during the siege of Jerusalem? (Ezek. 5:10)

TRUE OR FALSE

1380. Abner was the captain of Saul's host. (1 Sam. 14:50)

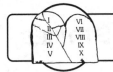

1238. Who buried Moses? (Deut. 34:5–6)

1239. Where was Samuel buried? (1 Sam. 25:1)

1240. Where were the bones of Joseph finally buried? (Joshua (24:32)

1241. Where was Sarah buried in the land of Canaan? (Gen. 23:19)

1242. It states that Moses was buried in the land of Moab; is the sepulcher of Moses known? (Deut. 34:6)

1243. Where was Solomon buried? (1 Kings 11:43)

1244. Jacob was buried in what land? (Gen. 50:13)

1245. Where was David buried? (1 Kings 2:10)

1246. Rachel was buried in what city? (Gen. 48:7)

1247. Which prophet raised a man from the dead after the prophet himself had been buried? (2 Kings 13:21)

This story involves wicked Prince Haman, the chief man in the court of King Ahasuerus; a Jewish man named Mordecai; and beautiful Queen Esther—Mordecai's adopted daughter and King Ahasuerus' wife.

Haman's advancement in King Ahasuerus' court made him a proud man who thought he deserved veneration from others, and he became extremely angry at Mordecai the Jew because Mordecai would not bow down and give him "reverence" every time he passed. His hatred and wrath spilled over onto all the Jews in the kingdom and motivated him to convince King Ahasuerus that the Jews were "diverse from all people. Neither keep they the king's laws," he said, and he contended that they ought to be "destroyed." He persuaded the king to issue a decree authorizing the destruction of all the Jews in the kingdom, and King Ahasuerus agreed to not only destroy them, but to cover the cost of their destruction from his treasury. The king gave Haman his ring to seal the order of destruction and said, "The silver is given to thee, the people [meaning the Jews] also, to do with them as it seemeth good to thee."

Haman immediately prepared an order of extermination, sealed it with the king's ring, and sent it in the king's name to all the lieutenants and governors that "were over every province" in Ahasuerus' kingdom. The order was devastating and irrevocable under their law. The book of Esther reveals how that order was overcome by Queen Esther and how she saved the Jews.

But for our next question, it is the description of how Haman's order was delivered throughout the kingdom that is important. A term in common usage today describes how Haman's order was delivered, so the question is:

1414. How were Haman's letters of instruction for the destruction of the Jews sent to the various rulers in King Ahasuerus' kingdom? (Esther 3:13)

Old Testament Fun

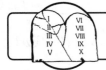
1062. What royal figure fell under Haman's extermination order? (Esther 4:8, 13)

1063. What was the name of the Israelite righteously slain by Phinehas? (Num. 25:11–14)

1064. What is the name of the fourth and youngest of Job's visitors? (Job 32:4)

1065. What is the name of the kinsman who was more closely related to Naomi than Boaz? (Ruth 4:1)

1066. Who named a son Gershom because he was as a stranger in a strange land? (Ex. 2:21–22)

1067. What were the names of Job's three friends? (Job 2:11)

1068. What was Sarah's name before she was called Sarah? (Gen. 17:15)

1069. Who was captain of the host of Israel under David? (2 Sam. 8:16)

1070. What was the name of Saul's youngest daughter? (1 Sam. 14:49)

1071. What is the name of God that describes why he requires us to worship no other god? (Ex. 34:14)

1072. What title did God use when he addressed Ezekiel? (Ezek. 2:1)

1073. Who gave the name of Obed to the first child born of Ruth and Boaz? (Ruth 4:17)

1074. What was the name of the god of the Philistines? (1 Sam. 5:2)

1075. Which of His names did God instruct Moses to use so that the Israelites would recognize that God had sent Moses to them? (Ex. 3:14)

1076. Who named Isaac? (Gen. 17:19)

1077. What was Abraham's name before he was called Abraham? (Gen. 17:5)

1078. What were the Chaldean names of Daniel's three companions? (Dan. 1:7)

1079. What was the name of Obed's son? (Ruth 4:22)

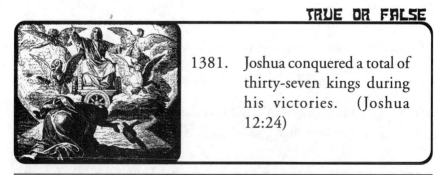

TRUE OR FALSE

1381. Joshua conquered a total of thirty-seven kings during his victories. (Joshua 12:24)

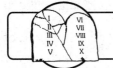

1080. How many times did Balaam smite his donkey before seeing an angel? (Num. 22:23–27)

    a.   1

    b.   2

    c.   3

1081. How many children were born of Bilhah, Rachael's handmaid? (Gen. 30:7)

    a.   2

    b.   4

    c.   6

1082. How many months did it take to complete the purification of Esther before she went before the king? (Esther 2:12)

    a.   18

    b.   6

    c.   12

1083. How old was Jacob when he went to Egypt? (Gen. 47:9)

    a.   30

    b.   130

    c.   230

1084. How many men did Zechariah prophesy would take hold of a Jew's skirt because they heard that God was with the Jews? (Zech. 8:23)

    a.   3
    b.   7
    c.   10

1085. How many times did Elijah call down fire from heaven to consume fifty soldiers? (2 Kings 1:10–13)

    a.   1
    b.   2
    c.   3

1086. How many sons did Aaron have with his wife Elisheba? (Ex. 6:23)

    a.   4
    b.   6
    c.   8

1087. According to the decree of King Darius, if you petitioned any god other than him for how many days, you were cast into the lion's den? (Dan. 6:7)

    a.   90
    b.   60
    c.   30

1088. Excluding the fowls, what number of each "flesh" was saved in the Ark? (Gen. 6:19)

    a.   7
    b.   4
    c.   2

1089. How old was Isaac when he died? (Gen. 35:28)

    a.   160
    b.   170
    c.   180

1090. How old was Jacob when he died? (Gen. 47:28)

    a.   137
    b.   147
    c.   157

1091. How many additional years did God promise Hezekiah that he would live? (2 Kings 20:6)

    a.   8
    b.   22
    c.   15

1092. How many times each year were Israel's men commanded to appear before God? (Ex. 34:23)

    a.   1
    b.   2
    c.   3

1093. How old was Josiah when he began to reign as king? (2 Kings 22:1)

    a.   22
    b.   16
    c.   8

1094. How many sons did Jacob have? (Gen. 35:22)

    a.   14
    b.   12
    c.   16

1095. Which year was the jubilee year under the Law of Moses? (Lev. 25:10–12)

    a.   40th
    b.   50th
    c.   60th

1096. David was the youngest of how many sons? (1 Sam. 16:10–11)

    a.   6
    b.   7
    c.   8

1097. How often each day did Goliath challenge Israel during his forty days of challenges? (1 Sam. 17:16)

    a.   each day
    b.   morning, midday, and evening
    c.   morning and evening

1098. So great was the wickedness of Judah, the Lord declared that from the prophet to the priest, everyone dealt in this manner. (Jer. 6:13)

    a.   sinfully
    b.   falsely
    c.   poorly

1099. How many days did Goliath challenge Israel before David slew him? (1 Sam. 17:16)

    a.   30
    b.   40
    c.   50

1100. How many times did Elisha stretch himself on a dead child to raise him? (2 Kings 4:34–35)

    a.   4
    b.   3
    c.   2

1101. How many sons did Naomi have? (Ruth 1:2)

    a.   2
    b.   3
    c.   4

1102. How much hotter than normal was the fiery furnace heated before Shadrach, Meshach, and Abednego were cast into it? (Dan. 3:19)

    a.   5
    b.   7
    c.   9

1103. Jethro chided Moses because he was _____ the people by himself. (Ex. 18:13–14)

    a.   judging
    b.   questioning
    c.   chastising

1104. How many days after Passover was Pentecost celebrated? (Lev. 23:16)

    a.   30
    b.   40
    c.   50

1105. How many of the Amorite kings were conquered by Joshua? (Joshua 10:5, 8)

    a.   3
    b.   5
    c.   7

1106. What was the number of Jacob's household that went to Egypt to be with Joseph? (Gen. 46:27)

    a.   70
    b.   75
    c.   80

1107. How many times did the Lord call the boy Samuel before Samuel answered? (1 Sam. 3:8–10)

    a.   3
    b.   4
    c.   5

1108. How many male children were born of Leah? (Gen. 30:20)

    a.   5
    b.   6
    c.   7

1109. What was the total number of Solomon's wives and concubines? (1 Kings 11:3)

    a.   700
    b.   300
    c.   1000

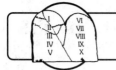

1150. What was Hananiah's Chaldean name? (Dan. 1:7)

1151. What was Gideon's other name? (Judges 7:1)

1152. Jacob's named was changed to what? (Gen. 32:28)

1153. King Mattaniah's name was changed to what? (2 Kings 24:17)

1154. What is Hadassah's more common name? (Esther 2:7)

1155. The Lord changed Abram's name to what? (Gen. 17:5)

1156. What was Azariah's Chaldean name? (Dan. 1:7)

1157. What was Mishael's Chaldean name? (Dan. 1:7)

1158. Sarai's named was changed to what? (Gen. 17:15)

1159. What is another name for Jethro? (Ex. 2:18–21)

1160. What was Jerubbaal's other name? (Judges 7:1)

1161. What was the former name of Zedekiah? (2 Kings 24:17)

1162. After Naomi returned to Bethlehem, she changed her name to what? (Ruth 1:20)

1163. What was the other name of Joshua? (Num. 13:16)

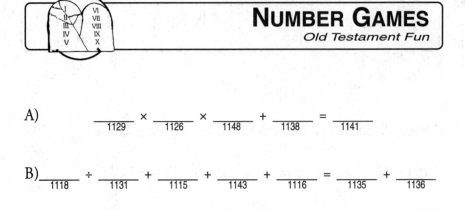

A) $\dfrac{}{1129} \times \dfrac{}{1126} \times \dfrac{}{1148} + \dfrac{}{1138} = \dfrac{}{1141}$

B) $\dfrac{}{1118} \div \dfrac{}{1131} + \dfrac{}{1115} + \dfrac{}{1143} + \dfrac{}{1116} = \dfrac{}{1135} + \dfrac{}{1136}$

C) Solomon had _____(1134) × _____(1111) + _____(1121) + _____(1131) concubines. He reigned in Israel for _____(1142) + _____(1133) years. If he had taken into his palace _____(1110) concubines each year for the first _____(1120) years, and _____(1115) concubines each year for the next _____(1127) + _____(1149) years, how many concubines would he have to take into the palace in the last year of his reign?

Answer: $\dfrac{}{1113} + \dfrac{}{1125}$

D) There was an unnamed Philistine warrior that went to battle in Gath. He was unusual because he had a total of _____(1124) fingers and _____(1128) toes. He also had _____(1144) brothers. All _____(1122) of them were born to the giant in Gath and fell by the hand of David and his servants. How many total fingers and toes did the brothers have?

Answer: $\dfrac{}{1123} + \dfrac{}{1112} + \dfrac{}{1130} + \dfrac{}{1145}$

E) $\dfrac{}{1114} + \dfrac{}{1119} = \dfrac{}{1132} + \dfrac{}{1137} + \dfrac{}{1139} + \dfrac{}{1149}$

F) $\dfrac{}{1146} + \dfrac{}{1140} - \dfrac{}{1147} = \dfrac{}{1117} \times \dfrac{}{1133}$

1110. How many chapters are in Micah?
1111. How many chapters are in Esther?
1112. How many chapters are in Zechariah?
1113. How many chapters are in Amos?
1114. How many chapters are in Isaiah?
1115. How many chapters are in Song of Solomon?
1116. How many chapters are in Genesis?
1117. How many chapters are in Malachi?
1118. How many chapters are in Ezra?
1119. How many chapters are in Deuteronomy?
1120. How many chapters are in 1 Kings?
1121. How many chapters are in 2 Kings?
1122. How many chapters are in Ruth?
1123. How many chapters are in 2 Chronicles?
1124. How many chapters are in Daniel?
1125. How many chapters are in Obadiah?
1126. How many chapters are in Zephaniah?
1127. How many chapters are in Hosea?
1128. How many chapters are in Ecclesiastes?
1129. How many chapters are in Haggai?
1130. How many chapters are in 1 Samuel?
1131. How many chapters are in Lamentations?
1132. How many chapters are in the Book of Job?
1133. How many chapters are in Jonah?
1134. How many chapters are in Leviticus?
1135. How many chapters are in Ezekiel?
1136. How many chapters are in Jeremiah?
1137. How many chapters are in Proverbs?
1138. How many chapters are in 1 Chronicles?
1139. How many chapters are in 2 Samuel?
1140. How many chapters are in Nehemiah?
1141. How many chapters are in all books of the *Old Testament?*
1142. How many chapters are in Numbers?
1143. How many chapters are in Exodus?
1144. How many chapters are in Joel?
1145. How many chapters are in Habakkuk?
1146. How many chapters are in Joshua?
1147. How many chapters are in Judges?
1148. How many chapters are in Psalms?
1149. How many chapters are in Nahum?

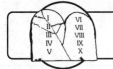
1164. Concerning the commandments Moses gave Israel he said, "thou shalt not add thereto, nor _____ from it." (Deut. 12:32)

1165. Be ye clean that bear the _____ of the Lord? (Is. 52:11)

1166. The Nazarites vowed not to drink _____ and strong _____. (Num. 6:3)

1167. Finish Ruth's statement: "Where thou _____, I will lodge." (Ruth 1:16)

1168. According to Isaiah: "The Lord give[s] you the _____ of adversity." (Is. 30:20)

1169. Finish: "Your old men shall dream_____, and your young men shall see _____. (Joel 2:28)

1170. The first verse of the book of Joshua addresses Joshua as Moses' _____. (Joshua 1:1)

1171. The Preacher declared that the conclusion of the whole matter was to _____ God, and _____ his commandments, which was the duty of man. (Eccl. 12:13)

1172. "Arise, shine; for thy _____ is come." (Is. 60:1)

1173. In Deuteronomy, the Lord described the chosen people as a _____ people, "above all the nations that are upon the earth"? (Deut. 14:2)

1174. Isaiah said, "Woe unto them that call evil good, and good
_____." (Is. 5:20)

1175. In Job's response to his catastrophes, he stated that the Lord
gives and the Lord takes _____. (Job 1:21)

1176. In poetic prophecy, Joel states that "the Lord also shall
_____ out of Zion, and utter his voice from Jerusalem."
(Joel 3:16)

1177. Isaiah: "How _____upon the mountains are the feet of
him that bringeth good tidings." (Is. 52:7)

1178. Isaiah's description of being sin-bound: "for the bed is
_____ than a man can stretch himself on it." (Is. 28:20)

1179. To complete Nineveh's repentance, the king ordered that both
man and _____ should fast. (Jonah 3:7)

1180. "Choose you this day whom ye will serve... but as for
_____ and my _____, we will serve the Lord."
(Joshua 24:15)

1181. Israel marched around Jericho but once each day for
_____ days. (Joshua 6:3)

1182. "The Lord is my _____; I shall not want." (Ps. 23:1)

1183. To ascend into the hill of the Lord, your hands must be
_____ and your heart _____. (Ps. 24:4)

1184. Because Leah had four children and Rachael had none, Rachael
_____ her. (Gen. 30:1)

1185. Isaiah said the earth would _____ to and fro like a drunk-ard. (Is. 24:20)

1186. The Lord is nigh unto a person with a _____ heart, and a _____ spirit. (Ps. 34:18)

1187. Joseph's blessing from Israel said he was a fruitful _____ by a well. (Gen. 49:22)

1188. "They have sown the wind, and they shall reap the _____." (Hosea 8:7)

1189. "Though the Lord give you the bread of adversity, and the water of _____, yet shall not they teachers be removed..." (Is. 30:20)

1190. "There is no _____, saith the Lord, unto the wicked." (Is. 48:22)

1191. "Saul hath slain his thousands, and David his _____ thousands." (1 Sam. 18:7)

1192. Isaiah said, the wisdom of their wise men shall _____. (Is. 29:14)

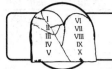
1193. What was Cain's answer when God asked him where his brother was? (Gen. 4:9)

1194. What did God tell Moses he would do to Pharaoh's heart when Moses asked Pharaoh to let Israel go? (Ex. 7:3)

1195. What is the first book of Moses called?

1196. Whose birthright did Jacob buy? (Gen. 25:31–32)

1197. The last chapter in Habakkuk is a prayer, but was directed to the chief _____ of stringed instruments. (Hab. 3:19)

1198. What type of language will eventually be returned by the Lord according to Zephaniah? (Zeph. 3:9)

1199. Mordecai refused to give Haman reverence and this type of obeisance, which made Haman angry. (Esther 3:2)

1200. What drove Elimelech, Naomi, and their two sons to move to Moab? (Ruth 1:1)

1201. Who mocked Elisha for being bald? (2 Kings 2:23)

1202. There are two historical books called "Kings." There are two other historical books written from another perspective. Can you name them?

1203. What famous ship was built of gopher wood? (Gen. 6:14)

1204. What is a common measurement of length in the Bible? (Gen. 6:15)

1205. How old was Aaron when he first talked to Pharaoh? (Ex. 7:7)

1206. What was the name of Jonathan's son? (2 Sam. 4:4)

1207. Under the Law of Moses, what was Israel not to kindle on the Sabbath? (Ex. 35:3)

1208. Esau sold his birthright to Jacob for what food? (Gen. 25:30, 33)

1209. When all Israel shouted outside the walls of Jericho, what happened? (Joshua 6:20)

1210. What did Ezra read to the people? (Neh. 8:3, 8)

1211. What did Ham see that caused Canaan to be cursed? (Gen. 9:22–25)

1212. What did Noah build first when he left the Ark? (Gen. 8:20)

1213. What were the reaper's instructions pertaining to Ruth's gleaning? (Ruth 2:16)

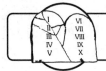

Match the questions on the left with the answers on the right. The solution is on page 269.

A. What is the chapter and verse of Joshua's "choose you this day" speech?

Ishmael

B. Jotham told the men of Shechem a parable about what tall flora? (Judges 9:8)

Isaac

C. Who was the first child in the Bible that was named before its birth? (Gen. 16:11)

Joshua 24:15

D. What coveted agricultural property belonging to Naboth did Jezebel say she would get for King Ahab? (1 Kings 21:1, 7)

Deuteronomy 4:2

E. What was the name of Nebuchadnezzar's captain of the guard? (Dan. 2:14)

Surety

F. What is the scriptural reference where Moses (like John) commands people not to add to his writings?

Vineyard

G. Who besides Abraham, introduced his wife as his sister? (Gen. 26:1, 7)

Arioch

H. What did Judah become for Benjamin in order to secure Benjamin's safety while he was in Egypt? (Gen. 43:9)

Trees

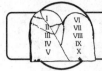

BODY PARTS CROSSWORD
Old Testament Fun

Solution on page 258

Across

3 In poetic verse, Isaiah describes the flesh of man as what green growth? (Is. 40:6)

7 The Lord's hand took hold of a _____ of Ezekiel's hair. (Ezek. 8:3)

9 The hand of Jeroboam dried up when he stretched it forth toward the man of _____. (1 Kings 13:4)

12 To put words into Jeremiah's mouth, the Lord put forth his hand and _____ it. (Jer. 1:9)

14 "The fathers have eaten sour grapes, and the children's _____ are set on edge." (Ezek. 18:2)

15 The Lord put forth his hand and touched the mouth of Jeremiah and put what in it? (Jer. 1:9)

Challenged by the Old Testament

16 The Proverb declares that the Lord hates "a proud look, a lying _____, and hands that shed innocent blood." (Prov. 6:17)

17 The complaining Israelites were to eat flesh, not manna, until it came out of what part of their faces. (Num. 11:20)

18 Isaiah conveyed the future requirement that every what, shall bow to God? (Is. 45:23)

19 Job states that after worms destroyed this corporeal entity, yet in his flesh would he see God? (Job 19:26)

20 Ezekiel saw bones connect and sinew and flesh come upon them. What was the last thing the Lord covered this structure with? (Ezek. 37:8)

21 Jeremiah said that Israel was in the Lord's hand, just as this material is in the potter's hand. (Jer. 18:6)

23 Joel prophesied that the time would come when God's spirit would be _____ out upon all flesh. (Joel 2:28)

25 As Ezekiel stood in the valley of dry bones, God asked him if the bones could do this. (Ezek. 37:3)

26 According to The Preacher, this will return to God when the dust (the body) returns to the earth. (Eccl. 12:7)

28 This is what Moses laid on Joshua to designate him as Israel's new leader. (Num. 27:23)

32 When Ezekiel prophesied to the bones, there was a shaking and the bones came _____. (Ezek. 37:7)

33 Satan smote Job with boils, from the crown of his head to the sole of what appendage? (Job 2:7)

35 "The _____ trieth words, as the mouth tasteth meat." (Job 34:3)

36 The Lord commanded Jeremiah to gird up his _____. (Jer. 1:17)

38 When the fathers eat sour grapes, the teeth of whom are set on edge? (Ezek. 18:2)

39 When Andoni-bezek was captured, what did they cut off of his feet? (Judges 1:6)

42 When Aaron was called to assist Moses, God said he would be to Moses "instead of a" what? (Ex. 4:16)

45 At their birth, Jacob's hand took hold of this part of Esau's foot. (Gen. 25:26)

47 When Eli saw Hannah praying for a son he could not hear her words, but could see this part of her mouth moving. (1 Sam. 1:13)

48 What part of Nebuchadnezzar's hands and feet grew to become like bird's claws? (Dan. 4:33)

49 In poetic imagery, Nahum said the clouds were the dust of the Lord's what? (Nahum 1:3)

50 Blood is the "life" of this according to the Lord. (Lev. 17:11)

Down

1 God commanded Ezekiel to set his face against whom in the land of Magog? (Ezek. 38:2)

2 David said his flesh would rest in hope because God would not leave his soul in this hot place. (Ps. 16:10)

4 Saul was taller than all the Israelites

from his _____ up. (1 Sam. 9:2)

5　The Philistines, after they had killed Saul, cut off his _____. (1 Sam. 31:9)

6　When God appeared to Abraham, Abraham fell on his what? (Gen. 17:3)

8　What was Ezekiel commanded to do with his hair? (Ezek. 5:1)

10　Ezekiel was carried by the spirit of the Lord and set down in a valley full of what white remains? (Ezek. 37:1)

11　Satan smote Job with boils, from the sole of his foot to what part of his head? (Job 2:7)

13　Nebuchadnezzar's hair grew like the feathers of what bird in fulfilment of Daniel's interpretation of his dream? (Dan. 4:33)

15　The third lie Samson told Delilah concerning how to eliminate his strength was to weave the locks of his hair with a what? (Judges 16:13)

17　As a sign to Israel, Joshua had the captains of Israel put their feet on the _____ of the five kings of the Amorites. (Joshua 10:24)

18　What "smote one against another" when Belshazzar saw the handwriting on the wall? (Dan. 5:6)

19　This "innocent" liquid was shed by Manasseh, and the Lord would not pardon him for it. (2 Kings 24:4)

22　God used this digit to write on the first stone "tables" He gave to Moses on Sinai. (Ex. 31:18)

24　Who uncovered the feet of Boaz as he slept? (Ruth 3:7–9)

25　God warned the Israelites in Jeremiah that they had taught their tongues to speak what untruths? (Jer. 9:5)

27　When a servant put his hand under this part of Jacob's body, it was a sign of the oath he took to go and select Isaac a wife. (Gen. 24:2)

29　The bones that Ezekiel saw in the valley were in what condition? (Ezek. 37:2)

30　Proverb: "The spirit of man is the candle of the Lord, searching all the inward parts of the _____." (Prov. 20:27)

31　The hollow of Jacob's thigh was "thrown out" of _____ from wrestling with an angel. (Gen. 32:25)

32　In poetic imagery, Isaiah said that God shall wipe all these away from the faces of the righteous. (Is. 25:8)

34　When Andoni-bezek was captured, what did they cut off of his hands? (Judges 1:6)

37　The Psalm declares that the law of the Lord is perfect, converting this part of a man or woman. (Ps. 19:7)

40　These two things are what Samson was avenging when he asked God to give him strength to destroy the pillars of the house he was in. (Judges 16:28)

41　Isaiah declared in poetic prophecy that at the day of the Lord, men's hearts will do this. (Is. 13:7)

43　Samson lost his strength because he cut this. (Judges 16:19)

44　The dead body that touched Elisha's bones was given this. (2 Kings 13:21)

46　Isaiah declared in poetic verse that the Lord's tongue is like what devouring element? (Is. 30:27)

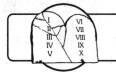

1214. The book of Job states that there is a spirit in man, and inspiration from God gives it what? (Job 32:8)

1215. Where is the book of Gad the seer? (1 Chron. 29:29)

1216. How old does the Bible say Enoch was when he was taken by God? (Gen. 5:23)

1217. When David summoned Uriah from battle, he did not go home, but slept at the door of the king's what? (2 Sam. 11:9)

1218. Who wrote three thousand proverbs? (1 Kings 4:30, 32)

1219. What nationality was Ruth? (Ruth 1:4)

1220. Who was the god of Ekron? (2 Kings. 1:2)

1221. When Hannah gave up her child, Samuel, she said she had _____him to the Lord. (1 Sam. 1:28)

1222. Zedekiah secretly took Jeremiah from a dungeon and asked him if there was any word from whom? (Jer. 37:17)

1223. What "captain" visited Joshua by Jericho? (Joshua 5:14)

1224. Where is the Book of Jasher located? (2 Sam. 1:18)

1225. How many concubines did Solomon have? (1 Kings 11:3)

1226. Which prophet told King Zedekiah that even if he declared the word of the Lord to him, he would not harken unto it? (Jer. 38:15)

1227. What was the disease that afflicted Naaman? (2 Kings 5:1)

1228. The book of Malachi is addressed to what nation? (Mal. 1:1)

1229. What is the name of Job's friend who said, "God will not cast away a perfect man, neither will He help the evil doers?" (Job 8:1,20)

1230. What did Elisha request before following Elijah? (1 Kings 19:20)

1231. What did Reuben offer to have slain if Benjamin did not return from Egypt? (Gen. 42:37)

1232. Which prophet was a herdsman from Tekoa? (Amos 1:1)

1233. What was the "half-shekel ransom" offered for in Israel? (Ex. 30:15)

1234. The image of Jeroboam's idolatry was of what form? (1 Kings 12:28)

1235. What two men was Nathan's parable of one little ewe lamb about? (2 Sam. 12:3, 7, 9)

1236. Where could the "avenger of blood" NOT reach his victim? (Joshua 20:4–5)

1237. What is the *Old Testament* name for the Sea of Galilee? (Num. 34:11)

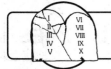
1248. Habakkuk asked the Lord: How long shall I cry, and thou will not what? (Hab. 1:2)

1249. Jeremiah asked God why the way of the wicked did what? (Jer. 12:1)

1250. Who said, "Whither thou goest, I will go"? (Ruth 1:16)

1251. Amos said the Lord God would do nothing but through his servants the what? (Amos 3:7)

1252. David cried: "My God, My God, why hast thou _____ me?" (Ps. 22:1)

1253. What did Hannah request of the Lord? (1 Sam. 1:11)

1254. In the trial of jealousy, what bitter fluid did a woman have to drink? (Num. 5:18)

1255. What famous queen visited Solomon and asked him hard questions? (1 Kings 10:1)

1256. Who asked Cain, "Where is Abel thy brother"? (Gen. 4:9)

1257. What question did Moses ask the Israelites after destroying the golden calf? (Ex. 32:26)

1258. What did Haman call casting lots? (Esther 3:7)

1259. What did it mean to cast "Pur"? (Esther 3:7)

It has been assumed by many people that the reference to a serpent speaking with Eve was nothing more than a symbolic story. However, the *Old Testament* records a story about another animal that was given the ability to speak to man. This story revolves around Balaam, a prophet from Pethor by the Euphrates, and Balak, king of the Moabites.

It seems that King Balak wanted Balaam go down and curse the people of Israel. But Balaam hesitated to do the king's bidding for when he asked the Lord what he should do, the Lord told him not to curse the Israelites, "for they are blessed."

King Balak again sent messengers to convince Balaam that he should go with them to curse the Israelites, and again Balaam asked the Lord what he should do. This time the Lord told him to go with the men, but to say what the Lord told him to say.

However, the Lord's anger was kindled against Balaam because Balaam had approached Him a second time when He had already given him His answer. So God sent an angel to block the way of Balaam's mount. The animal saw the angel and turned aside into a field, and Balaam smote the animal to get her back onto the path. The angel blocked the animal again, and Balaam smote it again. Finally, it records that the angel stood on a portion of the path that did not allow turning to either the right or the left, so when the animal saw the angel, she "fell down under Balaam." Balaam became angry and smote the animal again.

Then the Lord opened the mouth of the animal, and she spoke to Balaam. "What have I done unto thee," she asked, "that thou hast smitten me these three times." Then the Lord opened Balaam's eyes so he could see the angel, sword in hand, standing in the way. Balaam "bowed down his head, and fell flat on his face." In time, however, a humbled Balaam reached his destination and followed the Lord's instructions by blessing the Israelites instead of cursing them.

It is amazing to have an animal talk, but Balaam's reaction to this occurrence is even more amazing. He just spoke with the animal as if it were nothing out of the ordinary. This interesting *Old Testament* story now leads to our next question:

1415. What type of animal spoke to Balaam? (Num. 22:28)

In
Anticipation
Of Jesus

XI

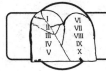

Match the questions on the left with the answers on the
right. The solution is on page 271.

A. Psalm 19:9 says the fear of the Lord is "clean," enduring for how long?

Psalm 19

B. Which Psalm praises the glory of God, and states that the firmament shows his "handywork?"

Wise

C. David declares in Psalm 23:5 that even in the presence of his enemies, the Lord has prepared what piece of furniture for him?

Work

D. Psalm 62:12 declares that God renders to every man according to his

_____ .

Truth

E. What is the longest Psalm?

Forever

F. "The testimony of the Lord is sure, making _____ the simple." (Ps. 19:7)

A table

G. In Psalm 22:18 David prophesied that men would cast these "chances" for Jesus' vesture.

Courage

H. Psalm 85:10 declares that mercy and this "real state of things" are met together?

Lots

I. David instructs us in Psalms to be of good _____ and wait upon the Lord. (Ps. 27:14)

Psalm 119

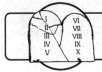

PROPHESYING OF CHRIST
In Anticipation Of Jesus

Solution on page 274

Across

3   Isaiah said that Christ would come in what kind of garments? (Is. 63:1)

4   Prophesying of the Savior, Isaiah said that He would divide this (it belongs to the victor) with the strong. (Is. 53:12)

6   In poetic prophecy, Isaiah said that Jesus would be _____ (injured) for our transgressions. (Is. 53:5)

8   Zechariah prophesied that Jesus would enter Jerusalem riding on this young animal. (Zech. 9:9)

9   Isaiah poetically called Christ the Prince of what desirable condition without war? (Is. 9:6)

10 Micah prophesied that Christ would be born in this city. (Micah 5:2)

12 Isaiah said that Jesus was a man of sorrows and acquainted with what emotion? (Is. 53:3)

14 In Zechariah, Jesus said he had received his wounds in the house of these associates. (Zech. 13:6)

15 Isaiah prophesied that the mother of Jesus would be a what? (Is. 7:14)

18 Isaiah said that with this form of His punishment we are healed. (Is. 53:5)

21 Isaiah said in poetic prophecy that for those who are bound, Jesus will open what place of incarceration? (Is. 61:1)

23 Isaiah referred to Christ as the everlasting what? (Is. 9:6)

24 In poetic prophecy, Isaiah declared that Jesus was brought as this animal to the slaughter. (Is. 53:7)

25 Isaiah declared that Jesus would be a man of what sad emotions, and acquainted with grief? (Is. 53:3)

26 Isaiah prophesied that Jesus would make His grave with the _____. (Is. 53:9)

27 Isaiah declared in poetic verse that this form of lying would not come from Jesus' mouth. (Is. 53:9)

Down

1 Isaiah prophesied that man would not desire Jesus because of his _____. (Is. 53:2)

2 Isaiah said that we esteem Jesus as stricken and _____ of God. (Is. 53:4)

4 In poetic prophecy, Isaiah prophesied that Jesus would be a stumbling _____ to Israel. (Is. 8:14)

5 Isaiah stated that as the sheep before the shearers, Jesus opened not his what? (Is. 53:7)

7 In poetic prophecy, Isaiah said that Jesus would be _____ with transgressors (a form of counting). (Is. 53:12)

11 Hosea prophesied symbolically that Jesus would be called out of what country? (Hosea 11:1)

13 David prophesied in poetic verse that the hands and feet of Jesus would be injured in what way? (Ps. 22:16)

16 Isaiah poetically describes Jesus as a what out of dry ground? (Is. 53:2)

17 Isaiah declared in poetic prophecy that Jesus would be wounded for our transgressions, and injured in what way for our iniquities? (Is. 53:5)

19 Generally speaking, does the prophet Joel describe the first or the second coming of Christ?

20 Zechariah prophesied that the price of the Lord's betrayal would be this many pieces of silver. (Zech. 11:12)

22 In poetic prophecy, Isaiah describes Jesus as growing up like a tender what? (Is. 53:2)

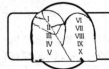
1260. Isaiah declares in prophecy that in the last days women will rule, and his people will be oppressed by whom? (Is. 3:12)

1261. Using poetic prophecy, Isaiah said that in the last days Judah would not vex Ephraim and Ephraim would not _____ Judah. (Is. 11:13)

1262. Isaiah said in poetic prophecy that in the millennium, a little what, shall lead them? (Is. 11:6)

1263. In poetic prophecy, Isaiah said that in the last days men would beat their spears into what? (Is. 2:4)

1264. In poetic prophecy, Isaiah prophesies that in the last days, swords shall be beaten into what? (Is. 2:4)

1265. In poetic prophecy, Isaiah states that in the last days, the vile person will speak what? (Is. 32:6)

1266. What weapons will be beaten into plowshares in the last days according to Isaiah's poetic prophecy? (Is. 2:4)

1267. Isaiah declared in poetic prophecy that in the millennium this type of animal shall dwell with the lamb. (Is. 11:6)

1268. In poetic prophecy, Isaiah said that in the last days children would be oppressors, and women would do what? (Is. 3:12)

1269. In poetic prophesy, Isaiah declares that the source of light during the Millennium will be whom? (Is. 60:19)

1270. At what age did Isaiah say a child would die during the millennium? (Is. 65:20)

1271. According to Isaiah's prophecy how many women will take hold of one man in the last days? (Is. 4:1)

1272. Isaiah declared in poetic prophecy that in the last days, what is to go out of Zion? (Is. 2:3)

1273. Isaiah declared in poetic prophecy that during the millennium, what will eat straw like the bullock? (Is. 65:25)

1274. In poetic prophecy, Isaiah states that during the millennium, nations shall not learn what, anymore? (Is. 2:4)

1275. Speaking of the last days, Malachi said, the day cometh that shall burn as an _____. (Mal. 4:1)

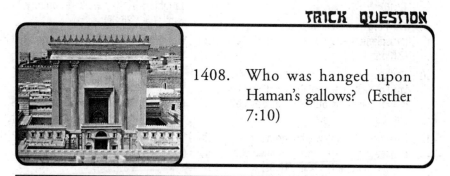

TRICK QUESTION

1408. Who was hanged upon Haman's gallows? (Esther 7:10)

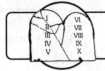

PUNISHMENT CROSSWORD
In Anticipation Of Jesus

Solution on page 277

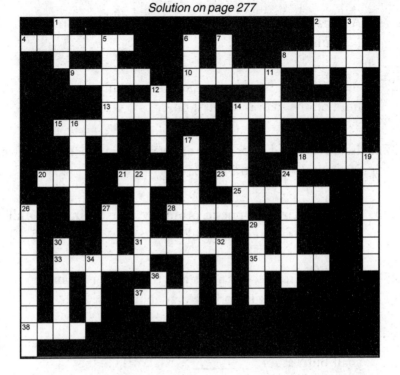

Across

4 The Lord punished Israel for forty years in the wilderness for breaching His what (another word for covenant)? (Num. 14:34)

8 This woman was punished with leprosy for speaking out against Moses. (Num. 12:10)

9 The Lord sent these animals among the transplanted Assyrian settlers in Israel. (2 Kings 17:25)

10 The chief governor in the house of the Lord punished Jeremiah by putting him in what ancient punishment device? (Jer. 20:2)

13 Fire consumed the two hundred and fifty princes that offered this perfumed substance improperly. (Num. 16:35)

14 To stop construction on the Tower of Babel, what did the Lord confound? (Gen. 11:9)

15 In Genesis, who does it say would be avenged sevenfold if slain? (Gen. 4:15)

18 God told the Israelites that they would eat the _____ of their sons and daughters if they walked contrary to Him? (Lev. 26:29)

20 Which prophet gave David a choice of three alternative punishments for numbering the people of Israel without the Lord commanding it? (2 Sam. 24:13)

21 Which son of Noah saw Noah's nakedness and was cursed? (Gen. 9:22–25)

23 Did Ahaz want to ask a sign of the Lord? (Is. 7:12)

25 The Law of Moses punished those with a "familiar" what by stoning? (Lev. 20:27)

28 How many of Ahab's soldiers (in addition to their captain) were destroyed by the fire Elijah called down from heaven? (2 Kings 1:12)

31 Who smote the men of Sodom and Gomorrah with blindness? (Gen. 19:1, 11)

33 In Genesis, who does it say would be avenged seventy and sevenfold if slain? (Gen. 4:24)

35 The Lord slew Nadab and who (sons of Aaron) with fire? (Lev. 10:1–2)

37 The Lord punished and consumed some of the complaining Israelites with what element? (Num. 11:1)

38 Because Zedekiah resisted the King of Babylon, the king put out his what? (Jer. 39:7)

Down

1 Ahab humbled himself before whom to avoid his immediate punishment? (1 Kings 21:28–29)

2 This is what God placed upon Cain because he killed Abel. (Gen. 4:15)

3 Which nation did God tell Habakkuk he would use to wreck vengeance upon the wicked? (Hab. 1:6)

5 What was the punishment for those who took accursed things from Jericho? (Joshua 7:25)

6 God punished Miriam with leprosy for speaking out against this man. (Num. 12:10)

7 How many of Judah's children were slain by the Lord? (Gen. 38:7–10)

11 Because of false worship, about three thousand men of Israel were killed at the base of what mountain? (Ex. 31:18; 32:28)

12 The state Uzzah was in after he touched the Ark of God. (2 Sam. 6:7)

14 Because Gehazi was unrighteous and took the gifts offered by Naaman, the disease of Naaman came upon him. What was that disease? (2 Kings 5:27)

16 Because they took the Ark of the Covenant and placed it next to Dagon, God smote the people of what city with "emerods"? (1 Sam. 5:6)

17 David was given three alternative punishments to chose from for numbering Israel without the Lord commanding it: Famine, fleeing before enemies, and what? (2 Sam. 24:13)

19 Because she ate the forbidden fruit, Eve was punished with sorrow in childbirth and would be ruled by what family member? (Gen. 3:16)

22 What was the name of the child of Jeroboam who died because of Jeroboam's wickedness? (1 Kings 14:1, 12)

24 What did Moses make the children of Israel do with the golden calf that Aaron made while Moses was on the mount with God? (Ex. 32:20)

26 What was the punishment of Queen Vashti for refusing to come when called by the king? (Esther 1:19)

27 Which member of Lot's family looked back at the destruction of Sodom and Gomorrah and was turned into a pillar of salt? (Gen. 19:18, 26)

29 This is what God punished the sons of Eli with for their sins. (1 Sam. 2:34)

30 What did the Lord bring upon Pharaoh's house because of Sarai, Abram's wife? (Gen. 12:17)

32 These were killed in front of Zedekiah before he had his eyes put out by the king of Babylon. (2 Kings 25:7)

34 This is what Jeremiah sank down into when he was let down into the dungeon. (Jer. 38:6)

36 This is what Ezekiel said would happen to the soul that "sinneth." (Ezek. 18:4)

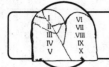
1276. The Lord told Jeremiah that even though both Israel and Judah cried to him he would not _____ to them. (Jer. 11:11)

1277. Through Jeremiah, God told Judah that her people could not hide their sins, even though they used much "soap," and washed with what? (Jer. 2:22)

1278. According to Ezekiel, when the wicked repent, all their former wickedness will not be what? (Ezek. 18:22)

1279. All the Lord required of the "backsliding" Israelites was that they acknowledge their what? (Jer. 3:13)

1280. What did God promise to do to scattered Israel if its people repented? (Neh. 1:9)

1281. Where did the Lord command Jonah to cry repentance? (Jonah 1:2)

1282. Because men's hearts were only evil continually, it repented the Lord that he had made what? (Gen. 6:6)

1283. Jeremiah declared that God was _____ of repenting? (Jer. 15:6)

1284. In Jeremiah it states that God will repent of the _____ He has promised, if you do evil. (Jer. 18:10)

1285. Who was angry when Nineveh repented?

1286. The blessing given to Judah by Israel promised that _____ would come through his linage. (Gen. 49:10)

1287. Which son did Israel bless to be a fruitful bough by a well? (Gen. 49:22)

1288. What did the Preacher declare was better than the day of birth? (Eccl. 7:1)

1289. How many times did Balaam bless Israel? (Num. 24:10)

1290. Benjamin's blessing from Israel said he would "raven" as what animal? (Gen. 49:27)

1291. When Jacob (Israel) blessed his son Gad, what did he say would overcome him? (Gen. 49:19)

1292. According to Isaiah, what will the "work" of righteousness bring to you? (Is. 32:17)

1293. In Issachar's blessing, Israel said he would become a what, unto tribute? (Gen. 49:15)

1294. Zebulun's blessing from Jacob (Israel) said he would be a haven for what? (Gen. 49:13)

1295. What was Eli's blessing upon Hannah for giving Samuel to the Lord? (1 Sam. 2:20–21)

1296. When Reuben was blessed by Jacob (Israel), he told him that he was as unstable as what? (Gen. 49:4)

1297. What was David promised that Solomon would have all of his days? (1 Chron. 22:9)

1298. What was the name of Israel's son through whom Shiloh (Jesus) would come? (Gen. 49:10)

1299. Which king did God promise to give fifteen more years of life? (2 Kings 20:1, 6)

1300. What would not depart from David's house as the punishment for taking Uriah's wife to be his wife? (2 Sam. 12:10)

1301. From which son did Isaac request venison before he blessed him? (Gen. 27:1, 3)

1302. Who spoke with Balaam and required him to bless Israel not curse it? (Num. 23:4–11)

1303. Naphtali's blessing from Jacob (Israel) said that he was like what animal let loose? (Gen. 49:21)

1304. According to Malachi, what must we do to open the windows of heaven for blessings? (Mal. 3:10)

1305. What blessing did Caleb have in his old age? (Joshua 14:11)

1306. Simeon's and Levi's blessings from their father Jacob said they would be scattered in what nation? (Gen. 49:7)

1307. What chapter in Genesis contains the blessings of Israel's twelve sons?

1308. What did God promise to make of Jacob's people while they were in Egypt? (Gen. 46:3)

1309. Who determined how King Ahasuerus would honor Mordecai the Jew? (Esther 6:6)

1310. Those to be blessed because of Abraham's obedience were himself, his seed, and who else? (Gen. 22:17–18)

1311. Ezekiel was told by the Lord that He would "deliver his soul" if Ezekiel did this. (Ezek. 3:19)

1312. Because Hannah asked the Lord for a son and her petition was granted, she named the child what? (1 Sam. 1:20)

1313. In Jacob's blessing upon his son Judah, he compared him to what animal? (Gen. 49:9)

AMAZING STORIES

Some of the most interesting stories in the *Old Testament* involve the creations of God in the heavens. This earth is precisely suspended in space. It rotates around its axis at enormous speed and travels around the sun once each year. The marvels of God's power are not only exhibited in His creations, but how He uses them. One of those marvels surrounds this question.

1416. As a sign that God would heal Hezekiah, which direction did Isaiah move the shadow of the sundial ten degrees? (Is. 38:8)

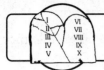
1314. Psalm: The judgments of the Lord are to be more desired than what precious metal? (Ps. 19:9–10)

1315. What did Jacob vow to give God in exchange for God's blessings? (Gen. 28:22)

1316. What does God promise he will have toward us, even though he may cause us grief? (Lam. 3:32)

1317. What did God bless Solomon with in addition to an understanding heart? (1 Kings 3:13)

1318. What did Phinehas receive for being zealous for the Lord? (Num. 25:13)

1319. Who was displeased with what David had done to Uriah? (2 Sam. 11:27)

1320. Whose judgment required that a baby be divided in half? (1 Kings 3:15, 25)

1321. Who received the king's ring instead of Haman? (Esther 8:2)

1322. Isaiah: The Lord gives you both the bread of adversity and the water of what? (Is. 30:20)

1323. How does Malachi say we deal, every man against his brother? (Mal. 2:10)

1324. Isaiah declared that those who committed the sins of Babylon would be burned in the fire as what? (Is. 47:14)

1325. In poetic verse, Isaiah declares that the Lord gives us the bread of what? (Is. 30:20)

1326. What happens to the righteousness of the soul that sins according to Ezekiel? (Ezek. 18:24)

1327. What was Jacob's reward for laboring seven years for Laban? (Gen. 29:23)

1328. Why did the Lord judge Eli's house? (1 Sam. 3:13)

1329. In Jeremiah, the Lord stated that Israel's sorrow was incurable because of the multitude of her what? (Jer. 30:15)

1330. Jeremiah said, get riches wrongfully and your end is to be a _____. (Jer. 17:11)

1331. Ezekiel said that if a man trusted in his own righteousness, and committed _____, his righteousness would not be remembered. (Ezek. 33:13)

1332. Jeremiah's girdle became marred and God said that as the girdle was marred, so would He mar the what of Judah? (Jer. 13:8–9)

1333. What cities did God destroy with a rain of fire and brimstone? (Gen. 19:24)

1334. When King Ahasuerus asked what honor had been given to Mordecai for his loyalty, what did his servants reply? (Esther 6:3)

1335. The Lord told Ezekiel that the righteousness of a righteous man will not deliver him in the day of his _____. (Ezek. 33:12)

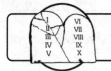

1336. What did Isaiah say would be created new at the Second Coming? (Is. 65:17)

1337. In poetic prophecy, Isaiah records that the Lord will wear red apparel at the Second Coming because He had trodden what by Himself? (Is. 63:3)

1338. Before the Second Coming, Joel said that the sun would be turned to what? (Joel 2:31)

1339. Micah states that when the Lord comes, the mountains shall be what, under him? (Micah 1:4)

1340. What does Zechariah say the words, "Holiness unto the Lord," would be written on at the Second Coming? (Zech. 14:20)

1341. According to Zechariah, what will happen to the Mount of Olives at the Second Coming? (Zech. 14:4)

1342. According to Zechariah, what will be written on the horses' bells at the Second Coming? (Zech. 14:20)

1343. Zechariah prophesied that the Jews would ask the Lord at the Second Coming, "what are these _____ in thine hands"? (Zech. 13:6)

1344. Isaiah said the day of the Lord shall come as a what, from the Almighty? (Is. 13:6)

1345. Joel said the moon would be turned to what, before the great and terrible day of the Lord? (Joel 2:31)

1346. Who will turn the hearts of the fathers to the children before the coming of the great and dreadful day of the Lord? (Mal. 4:5–6)

1347. Who did Malachi say would be sent before the great and dreadful day of the Lord? (Mal. 4:5)

1348. What did Isaiah say would roll together as a scroll as a sign of the Second Coming? (Is. 34:4)

1349. The Day of the Lord is described by what oxymoron in Joel? (Joel 2:31)

1350. In poetic prophecy, Isaiah declared that the Lord will come in garments of what color? (Is. 63:2)

1351. In poetic verse, Isaiah said the fire of the Lord would turn the dust into what substance at the Second Coming? (Is. 34:9)

1352. According to Zecheriah, the Lord shall be what over all the earth at the Second Coming? (Zech. 14:9)

1353. What does Isaiah declare will move out of its place at the Second Coming? (Is. 13:13)

1354. Zechariah prophesied that at "evening time" on the day of the Lord, it will remain what? (Zech. 14:7)

1355. In poetic imagery, Isaiah declared that when the Lord comes, what is to be beaten into "pruninghooks"? (Is. 2:4)

A lot of amazing women are mentioned in the *Old Testament* record. Our next two questions deal with some of them. The first question is a general one:

1356. What books of the *Old Testament* are named after women?

Piece of cake, right? Now we'll get more specific. The second question concerns a woman whose leadership position in Israel was truly unique in the annals of the *Old Testament*. Test your knowledge:

1357. Who is recorded as Israel's first and only female Judge? (Judges 4:4)

Now for one final, extraordinary question involving a situation that is singular in both the Old and the New Testaments:

1358. Who was the only prophet to perform a miracle, by raising the dead—*after the prophet himself had died and been buried?* (2 Kings 13:20–21)

Well, that's it. I hope you've had fun reading and answering the questions in *Challenged by the Old Testament.* I had a great time preparing them. Studying the scriptures is a serious business, but that doesn't mean you can't find enjoyment doing it. And that's what this book is all about—having fun while learning and cherishing the words of God.

The spiritual message of the *Old Testament*, whether it is plainly stated or occasionally cloaked in symbolism or imagery, leads to the coming of the Messiah and the eternal promises of the New Testament: God's gift of the resurrection and the opportunity for salvation for all mankind.

We owe much to the men and women who wrote the books contained in the *Old Testament*, and to the descendants of Judah who meticulously preserved them. It is my hope that you have enjoyed this drink from the well of Living Water.

— *E. Keith Howick*

Answers

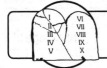

About Cities Word Search

from page 132

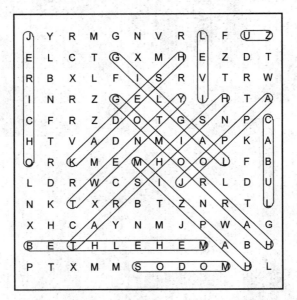

All About Mothers Match Game

from page 79

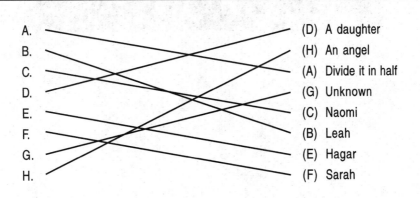

A.
B.
C.
D.
E.
F.
G.
H.

(D) A daughter
(H) An angel
(A) Divide it in half
(G) Unknown
(C) Naomi
(B) Leah
(E) Hagar
(F) Sarah

Body Parts Crossword

from page 228

Brothers and Relatives Word Search

from page 82

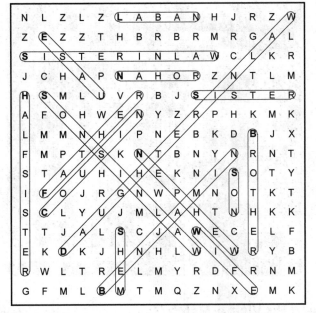

Covenant Match Game

from page 49

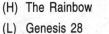

A
B
C
D
E
F
G
H
I
J
K
L

(H) The Rainbow
(L) Genesis 28
(E) Circumcision
(B) Wives
(I) Genesis 12
(J) It was a "curse."
(G) An "Ark of the Covenant"
(K) Children
(D) Jonathan
(C) The marriage covenant
(F) Our life for yours
(A) Beersheba

Daniel and His Vision Crossword

from page 188

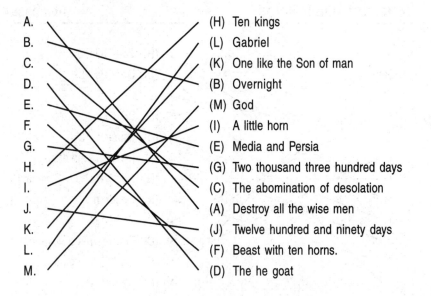

```
        ¹G O D    ²P      ³S
        O         U      ⁴E Y E S
        ⁵A N G E L      V       ⁶R   ⁷D
        T         S    ⁸J E R U S A L E M
⁹J U ¹⁰D A H  ¹¹T ¹²H R E ¹³E  N       M   N
        A         I     N   T
        R     ¹⁴B   M   ¹⁵D A Y S
    ¹⁶V I S I O N S           ¹⁷T
        U         O   ¹⁸F     E   ¹⁹K
  ²⁰W I S E     K  ²¹L I O N  ²²W A N T I N G
    I         S   F   U       N       ²³G
    N   ²⁴Q       ²⁵R O O T S       G       O
    E   U       ²⁶G     E  ²⁷F ²⁸A S ²⁹T E D
    ³⁰B E L T E S H A Z Z A R     R   W
        E         B           I   O  ³¹H
    ³²O N E     ³³D R E A M     O   N   O
                  I           ³⁴L I G H T ³⁵N I N G
                  E               O
                  L
```

Daniel and His Vision Match Game

from page 191

A.
B.
C.
D.
E.
F.
G.
H.
I.
J.
K.
L.
M.

(H) Ten kings
(L) Gabriel
(K) One like the Son of man
(B) Overnight
(M) God
(I) A little horn
(E) Media and Persia
(G) Two thousand three hundred days
(C) The abomination of desolation
(A) Destroy all the wise men
(J) Twelve hundred and ninety days
(F) Beast with ten horns.
(D) The he goat

David and Bathsheba Crossword

from page 66

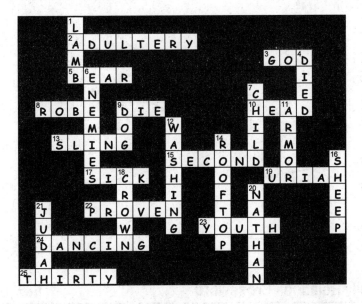

Death and Deception Word Search

from page 156

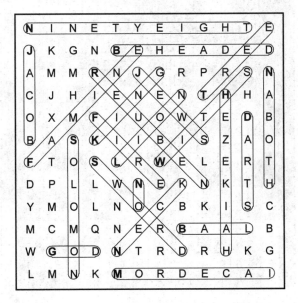

Easy Trivia Match Game

from page 120

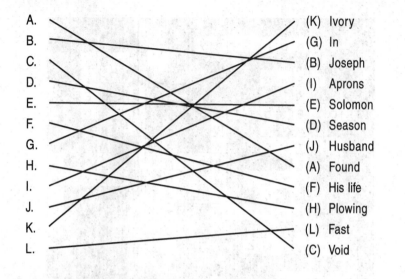

A.
B.
C.
D.
E.
F.
G.
H.
I.
J.
K.
L.

(K) Ivory
(G) In
(B) Joseph
(I) Aprons
(E) Solomon
(D) Season
(J) Husband
(A) Found
(F) His life
(H) Plowing
(L) Fast
(C) Void

Family Relations Crossword

from page 74

Fathers Crossword

from page 84

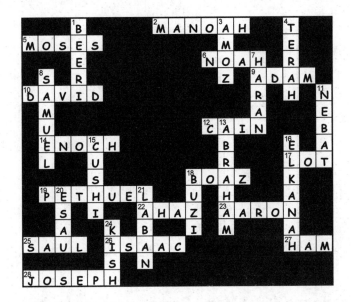

Flood Match Game, The

from page 27

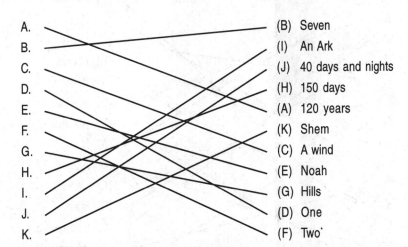

* The King James and Douay Reims versions of the Bible agree that Noah took seven pairs of the clean animals and two pairs of the unclean. Modern English translations of the Bible disagree on the number of unclean beasts taken by Noah.

Food and Drink Word Search

from page 104

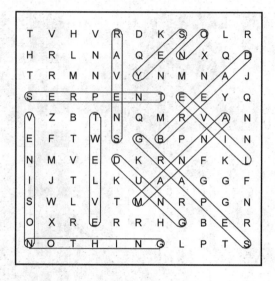

Husbands and Wives Match Game

from page 73

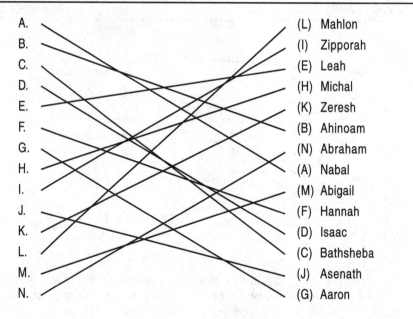

A.	(L) Mahlon
B.	(I) Zipporah
C.	(E) Leah
D.	(H) Michal
E.	(K) Zeresh
F.	(B) Ahinoam
G.	(N) Abraham
H.	(A) Nabal
I.	(M) Abigail
J.	(F) Hannah
K.	(D) Isaac
L.	(C) Bathsheba
M.	(J) Asenath
N.	(G) Aaron

Imagery Crossword

from page 200

Imagery Word Search

from page 94

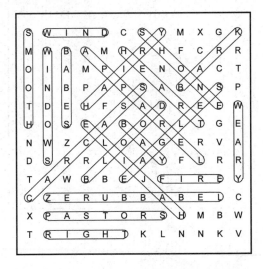

Israel's Mothers Match Game

from page 56

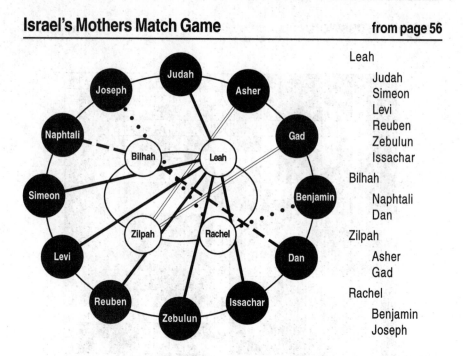

Leah

    Judah
    Simeon
    Levi
    Reuben
    Zebulun
    Issachar

Bilhah

    Naphtali
    Dan

Zilpah

    Asher
    Gad

Rachel

    Benjamin
    Joseph

Israel's Sons Word Search

from page 52

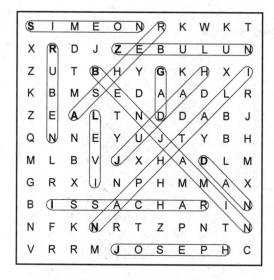

Job Crossword

from page 18

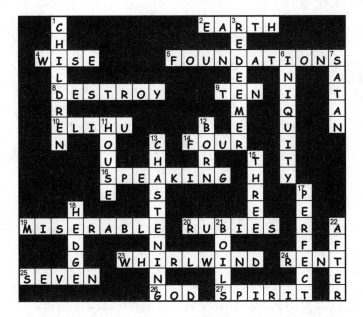

Jonah Crossword

from page 30

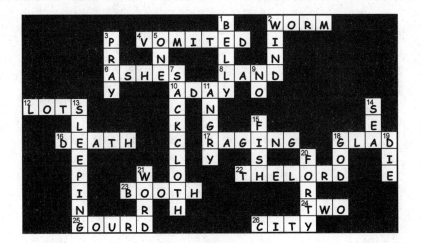

Joseph Word Search

from page 48

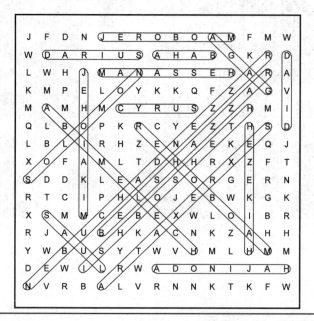

Kings Word Search

from page 142

Matches About Mothers Match Game

from page 184

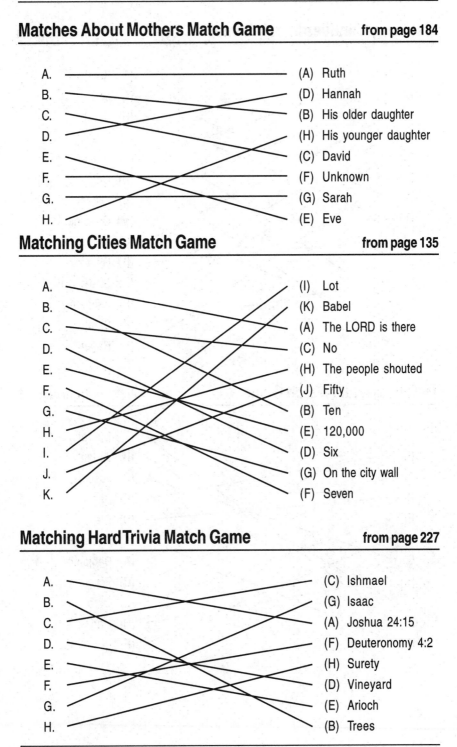

A. —————————————————————— (A) Ruth
B. —————————————————— (D) Hannah
C. —————————— (B) His older daughter
D. —————————— (H) His younger daughter
E. —————————— (C) David
F. —————————————————— (F) Unknown
G. —————————— (G) Sarah
H. —————————— (E) Eve

Matching Cities Match Game

from page 135

A. —————————— (I) Lot
B. —————————— (K) Babel
C. —————————— (A) The LORD is there
D. —————————— (C) No
E. —————————— (H) The people shouted
F. —————————— (J) Fifty
G. —————————— (B) Ten
H. —————————— (E) 120,000
I. —————————— (D) Six
J. —————————— (G) On the city wall
K. —————————— (F) Seven

Matching Hard Trivia Match Game

from page 227

A. —————————— (C) Ishmael
B. —————————— (G) Isaac
C. —————————— (A) Joshua 24:15
D. —————————— (F) Deuteronomy 4:2
E. —————————— (H) Surety
F. —————————— (D) Vineyard
G. —————————— (E) Arioch
H. —————————— (B) Trees

Matching Identities Match Game from page 60

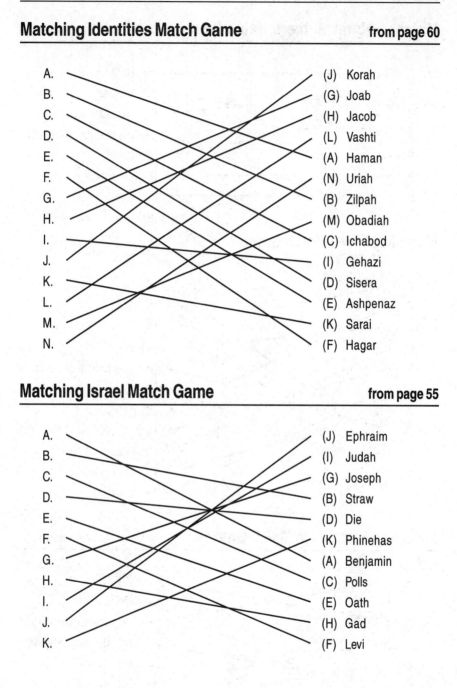

A.
B.
C.
D.
E.
F.
G.
H.
I.
J.
K.
L.
M.
N.

(J) Korah
(G) Joab
(H) Jacob
(L) Vashti
(A) Haman
(N) Uriah
(B) Zilpah
(M) Obadiah
(C) Ichabod
(I) Gehazi
(D) Sisera
(E) Ashpenaz
(K) Sarai
(F) Hagar

Matching Israel Match Game from page 55

A.
B.
C.
D.
E.
F.
G.
H.
I.
J.
K.

(J) Ephraim
(I) Judah
(G) Joseph
(B) Straw
(D) Die
(K) Phinehas
(A) Benjamin
(C) Polls
(E) Oath
(H) Gad
(F) Levi

Matching More Psalms Match Game   from page 237

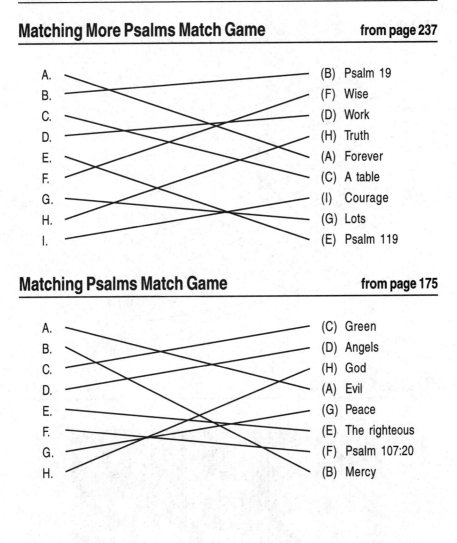

A.	(B) Psalm 19
B.	(F) Wise
C.	(D) Work
D.	(H) Truth
E.	(A) Forever
F.	(C) A table
G.	(I) Courage
H.	(G) Lots
I.	(E) Psalm 119

Matching Psalms Match Game   from page 175

A.	(C) Green
B.	(D) Angels
C.	(H) God
D.	(A) Evil
E.	(G) Peace
F.	(E) The righteous
G.	(F) Psalm 107:20
H.	(B) Mercy

Matching Time

from page 35

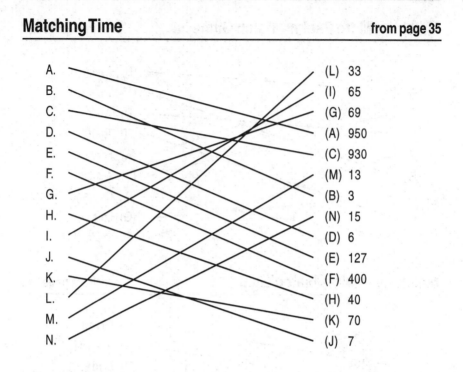

A.   (L) 33
B.   (I) 65
C.   (G) 69
D.   (A) 950
E.   (C) 930
F.   (M) 13
G.   (B) 3
H.   (N) 15
I.   (D) 6
J.   (E) 127
K.   (F) 400
L.   (H) 40
M.   (K) 70
N.   (J) 7

Miracles Crossword

from page 114

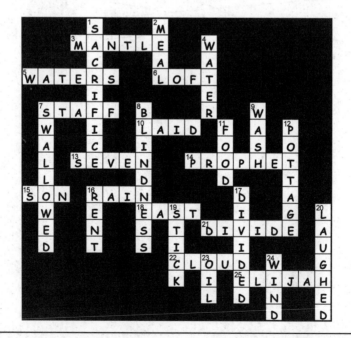

More Hard Trivia Match Game

from page 136

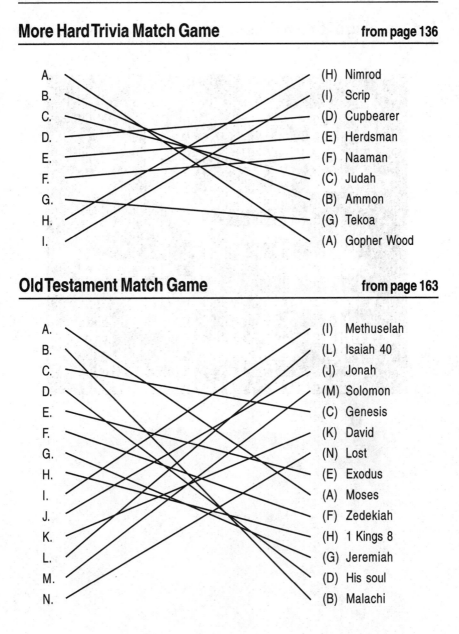

A.
B.
C.
D.
E.
F.
G.
H.
I.

(H) Nimrod
(I) Scrip
(D) Cupbearer
(E) Herdsman
(F) Naaman
(C) Judah
(B) Ammon
(G) Tekoa
(A) Gopher Wood

Old Testament Match Game

from page 163

A.
B.
C.
D.
E.
F.
G.
H.
I.
J.
K.
L.
M.
N.

(I) Methuselah
(L) Isaiah 40
(J) Jonah
(M) Solomon
(C) Genesis
(K) David
(N) Lost
(E) Exodus
(A) Moses
(F) Zedekiah
(H) 1 Kings 8
(G) Jeremiah
(D) His soul
(B) Malachi

Prophesying of Christ Crossword

from page 238

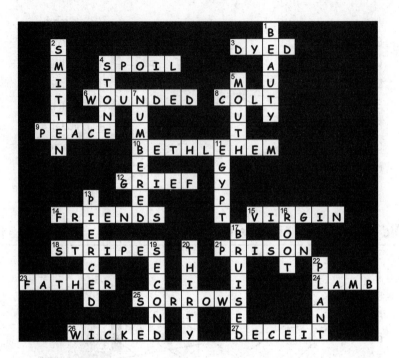

Challenged by the Old Testament

Prophets and Prophecy Crossword

from page 204

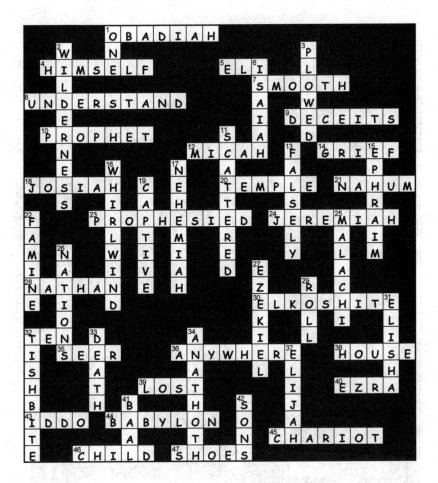

Proverbs Crossword

Punishment Crossword

from page 242

Rulers Word Search

from page 150

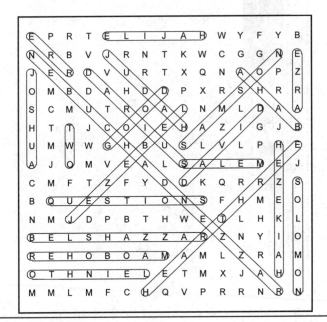

Search for Identity Word Search

from page 63

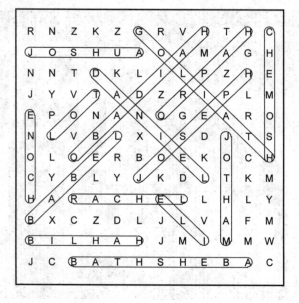

Search the Psalms Word Search

from page 166

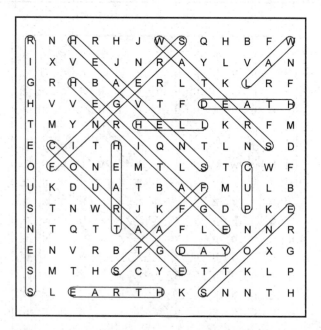

Challenged by the Old Testament

Searching for Fathers Word Search

from page 78

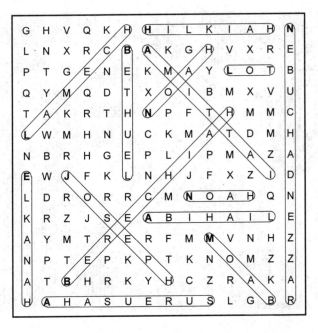

Seeing and Hearing God Word Search

from page 10

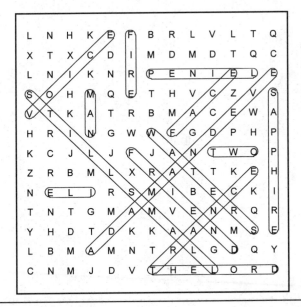

Signs and Visions Crossword

from page 108

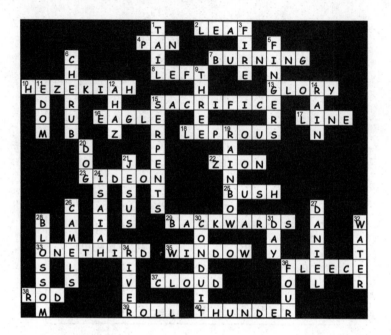

Symbolism Crossword

from page 194

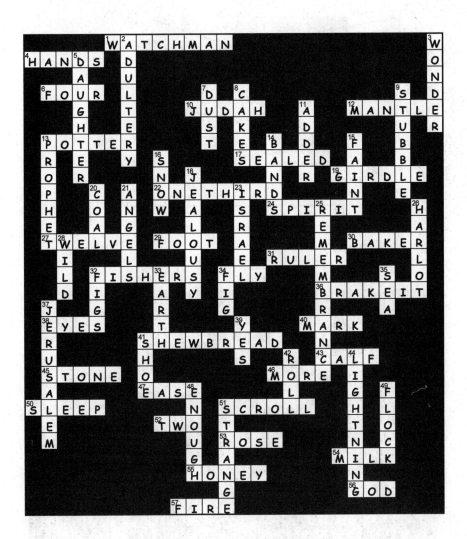

Ten Commandments Match Game

from page 93

A.   (E) Five
B.   (I) Eight
C.   (A) Three
D.   (C) Ten
E.   (H) Four
F.   (B) Seven
G.   (D) One
H.   (G) Nine
I.   (F) Two
J.   (J) Six

Women Crossword

from page 178

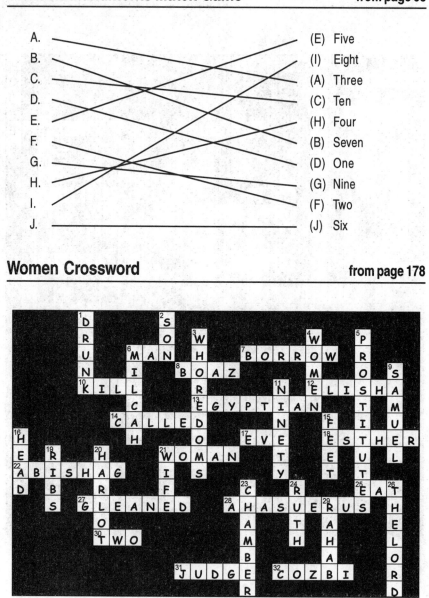

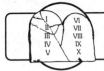

NUMBERED QUESTIONS

Answers to the True & False questions and Trick Questions can be found near the end of this list.

INTRODUCTION

1. The wood.

START

2. The tree of life and the tree of knowledge of good and evil.
3. She was Mordecai's uncle's daughter, or his cousin.

GOD

4. Chastening.
5. Sea.
6. Grief.
7. Cross over the river Jordan.
8. Jehovah.
9. Covenant.
10. Fire.
11. Foundation.
12. Jehovah.
13. Baal.
14. Mercy.
15. Prophets.
16. Esau.
17. Moses.
18. Flesh.
19. Light.
20. No.
21. Prophets.
22. The children of Israel.
23. Jehovah.
24. Humbly.

25. Waste.
26. Repented.
27. Earthquake.

CREATION

28. The fifth day.
29. Good.
30. Dry land.
31. Man.
32. He rested.
33. Lights.
34. The first day.
35. God.
36. Nothing.
37. The fourth day.
38. Waters.
39. The firmament, or heaven.
40. Earth.
41. All living creatures in the waters, and all fowl.
42. The dust of the ground.
43. The sixth day.
44. The waters.
45. Earth.

IN THE GARDEN

46. Eve.
47. Eden.
48. Cherubim and a flaming sword.
49. Alone.
50. Woman.
51. God.

Challenged by the Old Testament

283

52. Among the trees.
53. Dust.
54. Enmity.
55. The serpent.
56. The tree of life.
57. Before he transgressed.
58. Because he was naked.
59. Serpent.

SATAN

60. The second.
61. Morning.
62. A harp.
63. God and Satan.
64. Their eyes.
65. Earth.
66. One day.
67. The Most High.
68. The mouth of the serpent.
69. Destroy.
70. The gods.
71. Leviathan.

ANGELS

72. Oak.
73. Behind them.
74. The angel said his name was a secret.
75. A sign.
76. He produced fire from a rock.
77. Laughed.
78. A cloud of darkness.
79. His daughters.
80. Struck them blind.
81. Three.
82. Wrestled.
83. The Assyrians.
84. Two (1 Kings 19:5,7).
85. By the blood on their door posts.

UNIVERSE

86. Lightning.
87. Orion.
88. Stars.
89. Confounded.

90. A city.
91. The stars.
92. Job (Job 9:9).
93. Lucifer.
94. Light.
95. Joshua (Joshua 10:12).
96. Ashamed.

THE EARTH

97. The meek.
98. The heart.
99. Grass, herbs, and fruit trees.
100. Defiled.
101. Form.
102. Heaven.
103. Peleg.
104. Truth.
105. Remove.
106. Curse.
107. An earthquake.
108. Drunkard.
109. Thorns and thistles.
110. Burned.

WEATHER

111. Wind.
112. A vehement wind.
113. Elijah.
114. East.
115. Sea.
116. To die.
117. A little cloud.
118. It melted.
119. Rain.
120. Vehement.
121. A great wind.

WATER

122. The Red Sea.
123. The soles of the feet of the priests.
124. Still them.
125. The river Jordan.
126. Cisterns.
127. Moses struck the rock and water came out of it.

128. Elisha.
129. Marah.
130. Two and one-half.
131. The Jordan stopped flowing.
132. To heal them, or make them sweet.
133. Four.
134. Blood.
135. Women.
136. Elijah's mantle.
137. Walls.
138. To water the earth.
139. The Red Sea.
140. The river Chebar.
141. The river Jordan.

ROCKS

142. The Urim and Thummim.
143. His hand.
144. One.
145. His back parts.
146. Moses.
147. Twelve.
148. He broke them.
149. Each of the twelve sons or tribes of Israel.
150. Five.
151. The breastplate.
152. It filled the whole earth.

FOOD AND DRINK

153. Joshua and Caleb.
154. The knowledge of good and evil.
155. Bread and corn.
156. Forty days and forty nights.
157. Fruit (the forbidden fruit).
158. The ground was cursed.
159. Those that did not chew the cud but had a cloven foot and vice versa.
160. No.
161. The tree of knowledge of good and evil.
162. The woman, or Eve.
163. Bread.

164. Twice daily.
165. Meat and wine.
166. Jealousy.
167. Bread and flesh.
168. Fins and scales.
169. Bread, or manna.
170. The shew bread.

TIME

171. One week.
172. Babylon.
173. A year for each day spying the land of Canaan.
174. Methuselah.
175. A few days.
176. Before he was born.
177. His house.
178. Abib.
179. All night.
180. Midnight.
181. Half.

ANIMALS

182. Daniel.
183. Bees and honey.
184. It was let go.
185. He shut their mouths.
186. The tenth.
187. Elisha.
188. A dog.
189. A lion.
190. David's mule.
191. Three days and three nights.
192. Four (see The Flood Match Game for an explanation).
193. The Lord.
194. Samson.
195. Dogs.
196. A lion.
197. Black.
198. Bears.
199. Twelve.

PLANTS

200. Rods of green Poplar.

201. He would die.
202. The Lord God.
203. The cedars of Lebanon.
204. Nebuchadnezzar.
205. A raven.
206. Consumed.
207. The third day.
208. The dove.
209. Fig leaves.

FAMILY TREE

210. Jesse.
211. Ruth.
212. Sarai (Sarah).
213. Rebekah.
214. Abram (Abraham).
215. Solomon.
216. Isaac.
217. Jacob.
218. Boaz.
219. Bathsheba.
220. Judah.
221. Virgin.
222. David.
223. Shiloh (Jesus).
224. Leah.
225. Obed.

ABRAHAM

226. Lot.
227. Melchizedek.
228. Pharaoh and Abimelech.
229. Ishmael.
230. Abraham.
231. His son, or Isaac.
232. Righteousness.
233. Hebrews.
234. Once.
235. Eighty-six.
236. A famine.
237. One hundred years old.
238. An angel of the Lord.
239. Cast them out.

JOSEPH

240. Sold him.
241. One hundred and ten.
242. A goat's kid.
243. His (Joseph's) cup.
244. He wept.
245. Their money .
246. Ephraim.
247. Potiphar.
248. To buy corn, or because of a famine.

PEOPLE

249. Uriah.
250. Saul's.
251. Twelve.
252. The Lord.
253. One of the daughters of Canaan.
254. The Philistines.
255. David.
256. The mire.
257. The Gentiles.
258. Beauty.
259. The office of priest.
260. Solomon.
261. The children of Israel.
262. They became bondmen to Israel.
263. Egyptian.
264. Because he was perfect.
265. The Egyptians.

ISRAEL

266. Ephraim.
267. The tabernacle.
268. Egypt.
269. Abram, or Abraham.
270. Covenant.
271. Gods.
272. One-half shekel.
273. No.
274. Joseph.
275. Judah, Benjamin, Levi.
276. Thirty days.
277. Levi.

278. Manasseh and Ephraim.
279. Twelve precious stones.
280. Knowledge.
281. Remnant.
282. Accursed things.
283. A sin.
284. Famine.

JEWS

285. 10,000 talents of silver.
286. House.
287. Because Babylon would conquer Egypt also.
288. Benjamin.
289. Many became Jews.
290. The temple.
291. The land of the north.
292. Neighbor.
293. Cyrus.
294. Because they heard God was with the Jews.
295. He allowed the Jews to slay their enemies.

IDENTIFY

296. Moses' wife.
297. Ruth and Orpah.
298. Morashthite.
299. Simeon and Levi.
300. A prophetess.
301. Joseph's.
302. A widow.
303. Sanctuary.
304. Pharaoh's daughter.
305. Shadrach, Meshach, and Abednego.
306. Laban, or her brother.
307. A widow.
308. Lot's wife.
309. Gehazi.
310. A maid servant from Israel.
311. The Lord.

SAMSON

312. His wife (not Delilah).

313. Twenty years.
314. They put out his eyes.
315. Seven.
316. He tied firebrands between the tails of foxes.
317. As a weapon to kill one thousand men.
318. He pushed down two pillars thus collapsing a building.
319. With the jawbone of an ass.
320. A riddle.
321. They burned her.
322. Delilah.
323. She was a Philistine.
324. Ropes.
325. Dan.
326. A razor.

ESTHER

327. Scepter.
328. To save her life, and the life of her people.
329. Mordecai.
330. Haman.
331. To fast.
332. Death.
333. Banquet.
334. His life.
335. That he come to her second banquet.
336. The king's assassination.
337. His clothes.
338. He refused to bow to him.
339. Himself, or Haman.
340. Go in before the king.
341. Her nationality.
342. His order to kill the Jews.
343. Gallows.
344. Anything up to half his kingdom.
345. Hadassah.
346. Haman.
347. Ten.
348. Haman.

RELATIVES

349. Ephraim (Ephrathite).
350. Haran.
351. Esau.
352. Absalom.
353. Lot.
354. Saul.
355. She was the daughter of his father, but not his mother.
356. Miriam.
357. Sons.
358. Eleazar.
359. His sons-in-law and married daughters.
360. They died.
361. Son.
362. Leah.
363. Er.
364. A brother.
365. Tamar.
366. Jonathan.
367. Two.
368. Tamar.

HUSBANDS AND WIVES

369. Evil.
370. Seven hundred.
371. The Lord.
372. Curse God and die.
373. Leah, Rachel, Bilhah, and Zilpah.
374. His half-sister.
375. Sarai (Sarah).
376. Fourteen years.
377. Timnath.
378. Rebekah.
379. He died.
380. Eve.
381. The daughters of men.
382. One year.
383. Elisheba.
384. She became a pillar of salt.
385. Seven years of labor.
386. Uriah the Hittite.
387. Elimelech.

388. Keturah.
389. None.
390. Hannah and Peninnah.
391. Rachel.

CHILDREN

392. Jacob.
393. Mahlon and Chilion.
394. Esau.
395. Hophni and Phinehas.
396. Shearjashub.
397. His brother.
398. His sister.
399. Nadab and Abihu.
400. Isaac.
401. Sisters.
402. They called him a bald head.
403. Sneezed seven times.
404. Joel and Abiah.
405. Absalom.
406. Adriel, or her sister Merab.

MOSES

407. Spokesman.
408. God.
409. Eighty.
410. Forty days and forty nights.
411. Add.
412. Mouth to mouth.
413. Father-in-law.
414. To kill all male Israelite children.
415. The Lord.
416. Eliezer.
417. The Lord.
418. He fled from it.
419. Bulrushes.
420. His sister.
421. Three years.
422. Meekness.
423. A god.
424. An Egyptian.
425. Eloquent.
426. The angel of the Lord.
427. Prophets.
428. Aaron.

PLAGUES

429. Yes.
430. Yes.
431. Yes.
432. Yes.
433. The plague of darkness.
434. The frogs.
435. They died.
436. Fire.
437. Seven days.
438. Three days.
439. No.
440. The frogs.
441. Darkness for three days.
442. Turning dust to lice.
443. The death of the firstborn.
444. Hail stones.
445. Flies.
446. Locusts.
447. He killed a man and a woman.
448. Boils.
449. It became lice.
450. The plague of darkness

EXODUS

451. Cloud.
452. On dry ground.
453. The Lord.
454. Four hundred and thirty years.
455. To humble them, to prove them, and to do them good.
456. A cloud.
457. The firstborn.
458. A pillar of fire.
459. They borrowed from them.
460. An angel.
461. The sea.
462. They did not become old or wear out.
463. Seventy elders, Aaron, Nadab, and Abihu.
464. Water.
465. Trumpet.

466. They must wander in the wilderness forty years.
467. Nothing.
468. Murmured.
469. About Six hundred thousand.

SIN

470. They were not dressed, they were naked.
471. Defilement of the Priesthood.
472. Repenting.
473. Marriage outside the covenant.
474. By the laying on of hands.
475. David.
476. Man.
477. Gods.
478. Tithes and offerings.
479. The scape goat.
480. He killed his seventy brothers.
481. Five.
482. Fire.
483. His gods.
484. Cain.
485. Forty.
486. The woman, or Eve.
487. Poor.
488. The tree of life.
489. Fast.
490. Imagination.
491. The killing of Uriah the Hittite.

THE LAW OF MOSES

492. Leviticus 26.
493. A bill of divorcement.
494. The ark, or the ark of the covenant.
495. Yes.
496. He was stoned.
497. The "avenger of blood."
498. Leviticus.
499. At the end of the day's work.
500. Two or three.
501. The woman.
502. An inheritance.
503. Hilkiah.

504. Clovenfooted.
505. Your blood.
506. Death.
507. Death.
508. In righteousness.
509. Cud.
510. Death.
511. Usury.
512. An eye for an eye, etc.
513. Cut off.
514. Fish that had fins and scales.

MANNA

515. Quail.
516. Quail.
517. Coriander
518. Forty years.
519. On the sabbath.
520. White.
521. Wafers made with honey.
522. A month.
523. Six.
524. An omer full was preserved.
525. With hunger.
526. Twice as much as daily.
527. Flesh.
528. The Lord's bread.
529. Two days after the passover after crossing over Jordan.
530. It was filled with worms.

ARK OF THE COVENANT

531. Uzzah.
532. The two tables of stone.
533. Eli.
534. Dagon.
535. Two.
536. The Philistines.
537. He was struck dead.
538. Emerods and mice.
539. Emerods.

SACRIFICE

540. His son.

541. One hundred and twenty thousand.
542. Respect.
543. Jephthah's daughter.
544. Sons and daughters.
545. Where is the lamb?
546. God.
547. Abel's.
548. His daughter.
549. The sons of Levi.
550. The firstlings of the flock.
551. Baal.
552. Because God rejected it.
553. Burnt offerings.
554. The burnt offering.
555. The sons of Levi.
556. The fourteenth.
557. The fruit of the ground.
558. To obey.
559. A burnt offering.
560. He was to offer his son, Isaac, as a sacrifice.
561. Water.

TEMPLE

562. A cloud.
563. Jeremiah.
564. Food.
565. Cyrus.
566. Spirit.
567. A cloud.
568. The alter.
569. In the top of the mountains.
570. Two.
571. Fire.
572. Twenty-two thousand.
573. Solomon.
574. The glory of the Lord.
575. Oxen.

PRIESTHOOD

576. Blue.
577. Melchizedek.
578. Midian.
579. Zadok.

580. Aaron's.
581. Fifty.
582. Eleazar.
583. Offer an offering to the Lord.
584. 1 Chronicles 24.

FEASTS

585. The Feast of Purim.
586. Seven.
587. The death of the firstborn.
588. Pur.
589. The passover.
590. The fifteenth day.
591. Five.
592. Booths.
593. The Passover lamb.
594. The tenth
595. Convocation.

PROMISED LAND

596. Twenty years old.
597. Hebron.
598. Two (Red Sea, Jordan).
599. Caleb and Joshua.
600. Inheritance.
601. Because he failed to sanctify the Lord at the water of Meribath.
602. To prove Israel.
603. Caleb.
604. Grapes, pomegranates, and figs.
605. Thirty-eight years.
606. Reuben and Gad.
607. Two.
608. Every seventh year.
609. On dry ground.
610. Caleb and Joshua (Jehoshua).
611. Joshua.
612. It was done by lot.
613. Eleazar and Joshua.
614. Canaan.
615. Tithes.
616. Joseph and Levi.
617. The river of Egypt (Nile), and the Euphrates.
618. A cluster of grapes.

619. By the death of him that shed the blood.
620. Rent their clothes.

FALSE GODS AND PROPHETS

621. Hands.
622. Gall.
623. Men.
624. Lying words.
625. Heaven.
626. It fell before it.
627. Bless.
628. Iron.
629. Tail.
630. The Philistines.
631. Lies.
632. Money.
633. Divine, or remember his dream.
634. Everything.
635. Golden calves.
636. Balaam.
637. Cities.
638. Moab.
639. A golden calf.
640. Gold.
641. Heaven.
642. Nehushtan.

COMMANDMENTS

643. Bear no false witness.
644. Because they had been strangers in Egypt.
645. "Thou shalt not kill."
646. Ten.
647. Honor thy father and thy mother.
648. Thou shalt not commit adultery.
649. Look back.
650. Wife.
651. Do not covet.
652. Keep the Sabbath day holy.
653. "Thou shalt have no other gods before me."
654. Sum.
655. Day and night.
656. Moses.

657. The Lord.
658. Do not take God's name in vain.
659. Have no graven images.
660. Do not steal.
661. God.

GEOGRAPHY

662. Nebo.
663. The Plain of Jordan.
664. Nod.
665. Egypt.
666. Luz.
667. Egypt.
668. Edom.
669. Midian.
670. Sin.
671. Jericho.
672. Persia.

CITY LOCATION MAP

673. Shushan.
674. Sodom and Gomorrah. Genesis places these cities south of the Dead Sea. Many archaeologists today believe their ruins are now under water.
675. Jerusalem.
676. Bethel.
677. Shechem.
678. Zoar.
679. Bethlehem.
680. Nineveh.
681. Gibeon.
682. Jericho.
683. Anathoth.
684. Ur of Chaldees.
685. Joppa.
686. Ai.
687. Hebron.

JERUSALEM

688. A letter of authority.
689. Wept.
690. The wall.
691. Famine.

692. Two.
693. With dancing.
694. The word of the Lord.
695. Surrender.
696. Their King (the Savior).
697. Manasseh, Judah, Benjamin, and Ephraim.
698. Zerubbabel
699. The temple.
700. The Sabbath.

MOUNTAINS

701. Abarim.
702. Carmel.
703. Pisgah.
704. Noah's ark landed on them.
705. God.
706. Forty days and forty nights.
707. The Mt. of Ararat.
708. Thunders, lightnings, a thick cloud, or a trumpet voice (any).
709. Curse.
710. Hor.
711. The Mount of Olives.
712. Smoke.
713. Mt. Zion.
714. Flow down.
715. Eighty days.
716. In the top of the mountains.

KINGDOMS

717. "Chemarims."
718. Kingdom of God.
719. Assyria.
720. The Kingdom of Israel, or the Northern Kingdom.
721. Yes.
722. Nebuchadnezzar.
723. Jeroboam.
724. One hundred and twenty-seven.
725. Nebuchadnezzar's.
726. Assyria.
727. The kingdom of Israel, or the Northern Kingdom.
728. Media.

729. Isaiah 19.
730. He walked naked and barefoot.
731. Because Saul offered the sacrifice unrighteously.
732. Samaria (Israel) and Jerusalem (Judah).
733. Goshen.
734. The kingdom of Judah, or the Southern Kingdom.

GOVERNMENT

735. Christ's.
736. Reuben, Gad, and one-half of Manasseh.
737. Ten.
738. King.
739. Judah.
740. Jeroboam and Rehoboam.
741. He suggested rulers or judges.
742. Benjamin.
743. Manasseh.
744. Judah and Benjamin.
745. Ahijah.
746. The kingdom of Israel, or the Northern Kingdom.
747. Kings.
748. Judges.

ALL ABOUT KINGS

749. David.
750. Babylon.
751. Solomon.
752. Omri.
753. Artaxerxes.
754. Artaxerxes.
755. Rehoboam.
756. Abimelech.
757. Ahab.
758. Solomon.
759. Asa.
760. Zimri.
761. Hezekiah.

RULERS

762. Forty years.

763. That he would die.
764. "His soul."
765. His sons.
766. Samson.
767. Eleven years.
768. "God save the king."
769. Seven years and six months.
770. Nebuchadnezzar.
771. Because the Lord was with David.
772. Twenty-one.
773. Samson.
774. He was killed.
775. Rehoboam.
776. Their hearts melted.
777. David.
778. Two.
779. David.
780. Nebuchadnezzar.
781. The Lord.

WAR

782. Barak.
783. They fled.
784. David.
785. The front, or the most fierce part of the battle.
786. The Philistines.
787. Remnant.
788. To curse them.
789. An angel.
790. They were held up by Aaron and Hur.
791. Deborah.
792. To be Israel's ruler.
793. Spear.
794. Five smooth stones.
795. Joshua.
796. Goliath.
797. A noise of chariots and horses.
798. All nations.
799. He vowed that whatsoever came from his doors to meet him, he would sacrifice.
800. Moses holding up his hands.
801. An angel of the Lord.

802. Gideon.
803. Gideon.

DESTRUCTION

804. Jews.
805. Swallowed them.
806. Hail.
807. Prophets.
808. The sea.
809. Knowledge.
810. Brimstone and fire.
811. God.
812. Israel.
813. Levi.

DEATH AND DECEPTION

814. Skins of goat kids.
815. His firstborn son.
816. The Assyrians.
817. His sons.
818. An Amalekite.
819. Aaron's.
820. Hung it on the wall of Bethshan.
821. Esau.
822. Nebuchadnezzer.
823. Mother or Father.
824. Jacob.
825. Jonathan, David's nephew.
826. One hundred and ten.
827. Nine hundred and sixty-nine years.
828. The Shunammite woman's son.
829. The witch of Endor, or the woman of Endor with a familiar spirit.

OLD TESTAMENT TRIVIA

830. Rent (tore) it.
831. Two.
832. Water.
833. Jericho.
834. Selah.
835. One thousand and five.
836. Goliath's.
837. A Nazarite.
838. House.

839. Malachi
840. Thirty-nine.
841. The son of David, king in Jerusalem, or Solomon.
842. Forty-eight cities.
843. Genesis.
844. Ruth.
845. The Brasen Serpent.
846. Perish, perish.
847. Moses.
848. Woman (Eve).
849. In the king's gate.
850. Pastors.

KNOW YOUR BOOKS BEFORE

851. Zechariah.
852. Zephaniah.
853. Job.
854. Song of Solomon.
855. Hosea.
856. Exodus.
857. Isaiah.
858. 1 Chronicles.
859. Daniel.
860. Nehemiah.
861. First Kings.
862. Proverbs.
863. Jeremiah.
864. Esther.
865. Numbers.
866. Habakkuk.
867. Micah.
868. Psalms.
869. Lamentations.
870. Joshua.
871. Joel.
872. Amos.
873. Ezekiel.
874. Leviticus.
875. 2 Chronicles.
876. 1 Samuel.
877. Ecclesiastes.
878. Haggai.
879. Deuteronomy.
880. Judges.

881. Nahum.
882. Ezra.
883. 2 Kings.
884. Jonah.
885. Obadiah.
886. 2 Samuel.
887. Ruth.
888. Genesis.

KNOW YOUR BOOKS AFTER

889. Jeremiah.
890. Isaiah.
891. 2 Kings.
892. Ezra.
893. Deuteronomy.
894. Lamentations.
895. Zechariah.
896. Ruth.
897. Joel.
898. 1 Samuel.
899. 2 Chronicles.
900. Psalms.
901. Exodus.
902. Daniel.
903. Habakkuk.
904. 1 Kings.
905. Malachi.
906. Ecclesiastes.
907. Joshua.
908. Jonah.
909. Leviticus.
910. Micah.
911. Hosea.
912. Judges.
913. Nehemiah.
914. 2 Samuel.
915. Obadiah.
916. Job.
917. Haggai.
918. 1 Chronicles.
919. Song of Solomon.
920. Amos.
921. Numbers.
922. Esther.
923. Proverbs.

924. Nahum.
925. Ezekiel.
926. Zephaniah.

NAME THAT BOOK

927. "The First Book of the Kings."
928. "The Second Book of the Kings."
929. Numbers.
930. "The Second Book of the Kings."
931. The Book of Psalms.
932. The Lamentations of Jeremiah.
933. Ecclesiastes.
934. Numbers.
935. "The Second Book of the Kings, Commonly Called, The Fourth Book of the Kings."
936. Deuteronomy.
937. Jasher.
938. "The Second Book of Samuel."
939. Leviticus.
940. The Third Book of the Kings.
941. "The First Book of Samuel, Otherwise Called, The First Book of the Kings."
942. "The First Book of the Kings, Commonly Called, The Third Book of the Kings."
943. "The Second Book of Samuel, Otherwise Called, The Second Book of the Kings."
944. "The First Book of the Kings."
945. Exodus.

DEFINITIONS

946. The earth.
947. Isaiah 58.
948. A priest of Baal.
949. Time.
950. Die.
951. Sorrow.
952. Prophet.
953. The congregation of the righteous.
954. Sin.
955. Vanity.

956. Birth.
957. His commandments.
958. Priest.
959. A good name.
960. Sacrifice.

CLOTHING

961. They did not become old.
962. Aprons.
963. None.
964. Coats of skin.
965. Aaron.
966. Leather.
967. Each other's clothing.
968. White as snow.
969. Clothes.
970. Robe.
971. Sackcloth.
972. Holy ground.

UNIQUE FINE POINTS

973. Red.
974. Stone tablets.
975. Hair.
976. Steel.
977. The temple.
978. To be cast into a fiery furnace.
979. A "blessing."
980. Saul's.
981. Wroth.
982. The Spirit.
983. Fire destroyed them.
984. Woman.
985. Himself.
986. Pray for them.
987. A nail was driven through his temples.
988. He had six fingers and six toes.
989. By a whirlwind.
990. The guards of Shadrach, Meshach, and Abednego.
991. Elisha.
992. "I cannot; for it is sealed."
993. He was called a Jew.

994. A chariot of fire, drawn by horses of fire.
995. The Lord.
996. Drink no wine and don't cut your hair.

THE MAN-IMAGE DREAM

997. Iron and clay.
998. Brass.
999. Gold.
1000. Terrible.
1001. Iron.
1002. Silver.

DREAMS

1003. The chief butler and the chief baker.
1004. A ladder.
1005. The butler.
1006. He worshiped Daniel.
1007. Him (Nebuchadnezzar).
1008. He forgot it.
1009. Bethel.
1010. A tree.
1011. The baker.
1012. Joseph.
1013. The Lord.

VISIONS

1014. Man, lion, ox, and eagle.
1015. Red.
1016. The Son of God.
1017. A curse.
1018. Two anointed ones, or prophets.
1019. Eli.
1020. The four spirits of the heavens.
1021. Burden.
1022. A whirlwind.
1023. Two angels.
1024. Fiery chariots.
1025. The promised land.
1026. White.
1027. Fire.
1028. Six.

ELIJAH

1029. Mantle.
1030. Four hundred.
1031. Two.
1032. Four hundred and fifty.
1033. He killed them.
1034. The rain.
1035. 1 Kings 17.
1036. He raised her son from the dead.
1037. As an hairy man.
1038. He asked Elijah not to destroy him.
1039. An angel.
1040. The feast of harvest, weeks, or Pentecost.
1041. The dogs would lick his blood.
1042. 1 Kings 17.

PROPHECY AND PROPHETS

1043. Isaiah 2:2–3; Micah 4:1–2.
1044. Eli.
1045. Jeremiah.
1046. Only him.
1047. Nathan the prophet.
1048. Elijah.
1049. The Lord.
1050. Four.
1051. Nathan.
1052. Elijah.
1053. Elijah taken by the chariot of fire.
1054. Elijah.
1055. All Israel.
1056. There would be no rain but on his (Elijah's) word.
1057. A wife and children.
1058. A false prophet.
1059. Jeremiah (Jer 36:27).
1060. Nations.
1061. Lost.

NAMES

1062. Esther.
1063. Zimri.
1064. Elihu.

1065. His name is not recorded.
1066. Moses.
1067. Eliphaz, Bildad, Zophar.
1068. Sarai.
1069. Joab.
1070. Michal.
1071. Jealous.
1072. Son of man.
1073. The women who were neighbors of Naomi.
1074. Dagon.
1075. "I AM."
1076. God.
1077. Abram.
1078. Shadrach, Meshach, and Abed-nego.
1079. Jesse.

MULTIPLE CHOICE

1080. Three.
1081. Two.
1082. Twelve months.
1083. One hundred and thirty years.
1084. Ten.
1085. Two.
1086. Four.
1087. Thirty.
1088. Two.
1089. One hundred and eighty years.
1090. One hundred and forty-seven.
1091. Fifteen.
1092. Three.
1093. Eight.
1094. Twelve.
1095. The fiftieth year.
1096. Eight.
1097. Each morning and each evening.
1098. Falsely.
1099. Forty.
1100. Two.
1101. Two.
1102. Seven times.
1103. Because he was judging all the people by himself.
1104. Fifty.

1105. Five.
1106. Seventy.
1107. Four times
1108. Six.
1109. One thousand.

NUMBER GAMES

1110. Seven.
1111. Ten.
1112. Fourteen.
1113. Nine.
1114. Sixty-six.
1115. Eight.
1116. Fifty.
1117. Four.
1118. Ten.
1119. Thirty-four.
1120. Twenty-two.
1121. Twenty-five.
1122. Four.
1123. Thirty-six.
1124. Twelve.
1125. One.
1126. Three.
1127. Fourteen.
1128. Twelve.
1129. Two.
1130. Thirty-one.
1131. Five.
1132. Forty-two.
1133. Four.
1134. Twenty-seven.
1135. Forty-eight.
1136. Fifty-two.
1137. Thirty-one.
1138. Twenty-nine.
1139. Twenty-four.
1140. Thirteen.
1141. Nine hundred and twenty-nine.
1142. Thirty-six.
1143. Forty.
1144. Three.
1145. Three.
1146. Twenty-four.
1147. Twenty-one.

1148. One hundred and fifty.
1149. Three.

NAME CHANGES

1150. Shadrach.
1151. Jerubbaal.
1152. Israel.
1153. Zedekiah.
1154. Esther.
1155. Abraham.
1156. Abednego.
1157. Meshach.
1158. Sarah.
1159. Reuel.
1160. Gideon.
1161. Mattaniah.
1162. Mara.
1163. Oshea.

FILL IN THE BLANK

1164. Diminish.
1165. Vessels.
1166. Wine, drink.
1167. Lodgest.
1168. Bread.
1169. Dreams, visions.
1170. Minister.
1171. Fear, keep.
1172. Light.
1173. A peculiar people.
1174. Evil.
1175. Away.
1176. Roar.
1177. Beautiful.
1178. Shorter.
1179. Beast.
1180. Me, house.
1181. Six.
1182. Shepherd.
1183. Clean, pure.
1184. Envied.
1185. Reel.
1186. Broken, contrite.
1187. Bough.
1188. Whirlwind.

1189. Affliction.
1190. Peace.
1191. Ten.
1192. Perish.

EASY TRIVIA

1193. "Am I my brother's keeper?"
1194. Harden it.
1195. Genesis.
1196. Esau's, or his brother's.
1197. Singer.
1198. A pure one.
1199. Bow to him.
1200. A famine.
1201. Little children.
1202. First and Second Chronicles.
1203. Noah's ark.
1204. A cubit.
1205. Eighty-three years.
1206. Mephibosheth.
1207. A fire.
1208. Red pottage.
1209. The wall fell down.
1210. The book of the law.
1211. Noah's nakedness.
1212. An altar.
1213. Let some of the grain fall on purpose.

HARD TRIVIA

1214. Understanding.
1215. No one knows.
1216. Three hundred and sixty-five.
1217. House.
1218. Solomon.
1219. Of Moab.
1220. Baalzebub.
1221. Lent.
1222. The Lord.
1223. The captain of the host of the Lord.
1224. Unknown.
1225. Three hundred.
1226. Jeremiah.
1227. Leprosy.

1228. Israel.
1229. Bildad
1230. To kiss his father and mother goodbye.
1231. His two sons.
1232. Amos.
1233. The atonement for one's soul.
1234. He worshiped two golden calves.
1235. David and Uriah.
1236. Any city of refuge.
1237. The Sea of Chinnereth.

BURIALS

1238. God.
1239. At Ramah.
1240. Shechem.
1241. Hebron.
1242. No.
1243. In the city of David.
1244. Canaan.
1245. The city of David (Jerusalem).
1246. Ephrath, or Bethlehem.
1247. Elisha.

QUESTIONS

1248. Hear.
1249. Prospered.
1250. Ruth.
1251. Prophets.
1252. Forsaken.
1253. To have a son.
1254. Water.
1255. The queen of Sheba.
1256. The Lord.
1257. "Who is on the Lord's side?"
1258. Pur.
1259. To cast lots.

THE LAST DAYS

1260. Children.
1261. Envy.
1262. Child.
1263. Pruninghooks.
1264. Plowshares.
1265. Villainy.

1266. Swords.
1267. Wolf.
1268. Rule.
1269. The Lord.
1270. One hundred.
1271. Seven.
1272. The law.
1273. The lion.
1274. War.
1275. Oven.

REPENTANCE

1276. Harken.
1277. Nitre.
1278. Mentioned.
1279. Iniquity.
1280. Gather it.
1281. Nineveh.
1282. Man.
1283. Weary.
1284. The good he has promised.
1285. Jonah (Jonah 4:1).

BLESSINGS

1286. Shiloh, or Christ.
1287. Joseph.
1288. The day of death.
1289. Three.
1290. Wolf.
1291. A troop.
1292. Peace.
1293. Servant.
1294. Ships.
1295. She had more children.
1296. Water.
1297. Peace and quietness.
1298. Judah.
1299. Hezekiah.
1300. The sword.
1301. Esau.
1302. God.
1303. Hind.
1304. Pay tithing.
1305. His youthful strength.
1306. Israel.

1307. Genesis 49.
1308. A great nation.
1309. Haman.
1310. All nations.
1311. Warn the wicked.
1312. Samuel.
1313. A lion's whelp.

JUDGMENT AND REWARD

1314. Gold.
1315. One tenth of all.
1316. Compassion.
1317. Riches and honor.
1318. The priesthood.
1319. The Lord.
1320. Solomon's.
1321. Mordecai.
1322. Affliction.
1323. Treacherously.
1324. Stubble.
1325. Adversity.
1326. He dies.
1327. Leah.
1328. Because Eli did not correct his sons' sins.
1329. Iniquities.
1330. A fool.
1331. Iniquity.
1332. Pride.
1333. Sodom and Gomorrah.
1334. Nothing.
1335. Transgression.

SECOND COMING

1336. The heaven and earth.
1337. The winepress.
1338. Darkness.
1339. Molten.
1340. The bells of the horses.
1341. It will cleave in two.
1342. "Holiness unto the Lord."
1343. Wounds.
1344. Destruction.
1345. Blood.
1346. Elijah.

1347. Elijah.
1348. The heavens.
1349. "Great and terrible."
1350. Red.
1351. Brimstone.
1352. King.
1353. The earth.
1354. It will be light.
1355. Spears.

FINALE

1356. Ruth and Esther.
1357. Deborah.
1358. Elisha.

TRUE/FALSE

1359. False (he commanded the sun and moon to stand still).
1360. False (the brook Cherith).
1361. True.
1362. True.
1363. True.
1364. False (Three).
1365. True.
1366. True.
1367. False (they only used trumpets).
1368. False (he requested golden earrings).
1369. False (three hundred men).
1370. False (Ahab disguised himself).
1371. False (he stretched himself three times upon him).
1372. True.
1373. True (he is also called Jethro [Ex. 2:18], and Raguel [Num. 10:29]).
1374. False (it was watered with a mist).
1375. True.
1376. True.
1377. True.
1378. False (bonds and yokes).
1379. False (he cast in a tree).

1380. True.
1381. False (Thirty-one).

TRICK QUESTIONS

1382. To wash in.
1383. Him, him.
1384. A fourth kingdom.
1385. Nineveh.
1386. Twenty-five.
1387. Good.
1388. Hosea.
1389. A wheel.
1390. Two.
1391. Amos.
1392. Twenty.
1393. Twenty-four.
1394. Vanity.
1395. Micah.
1396. The Book of the Acts of Solomon.
1397. None.
1398. Lost.
1399. Nun.
1400. None.
1401. The Lord.
1402. Lighter.
1403. The donkey.
1404. Peace.
1405. Saul.
1406. Elisha.
1407. Adam.
1408. Haman.

AMAZING STORIES

1409. Scapegoat.
1410. Tare them.
1411. The house of Israel.
1412. Baal.
1413. It swam.
1414. "By posts."
1415. An ass or donkey.
1416. Backward.